BE STILL, MY SOUL

Be Still My Soul

by
ELIZABETH URCH

Author of

Queen of the Manse
Ladders up to Heaven:
Christmas
Friendship
Sorrow
Worship

ARTHUR JAMES LIMITED
ONE CRANBOURNE ROAD, LONDON N10 2BT

First Edition 1964
Paperback Edition 1969
Reprinted 1972
Reprinted 1978
Reprinted 1987

© Elizabeth Urch, 1964

All rights reserved by Arthur James Limited, London

ISBN 0 85305 173 9

MADE AND PRINTED IN GREAT BRITAIN BY
THE GUERNSEY PRESS CO. LTD, GUERNSEY, CHANNEL ISLANDS

DEDICATION

To our three children,
Michael, Maureen and Rosalind,
who have so bravely helped
me bear my sorrow,
and to the memory of Walter,
a dear husband and father.

A Tribute

from

Catherine Marshall

FOR MYSELF, I find those books in the religious field most helpful which are written not from theory nor from theological interpretations, but out of experience. Such a book is Elizabeth Urch's *Be Still, My Soul*. It is a true story, movingly told.

Be Still, My Soul offers inspiration as well as practical help for all those who grapple with ultimate questions of life and death, and with the painful re-adjustments of bereavement.

I heartily recommend Elizabeth Urch's book.

CATHERINE MARSHALL

Chappaqua, New York.

Foreword

WHEN WE BEGAN broadcasting the *Silver Lining* programme fifteen years ago, we said that our object was
to try to bring comfort and help to those in sorrow, sickness
or need, and this, of course, included bereavement.

Mrs. Elizabeth Urch, who was tragically bereaved and left
with a young family to provide for and educate, has spoken
several times in the *Silver Lining* about her experiences, and
told us how as a Christian she accepted the situation and
triumphed over it.

In this little book *Be Still, My Soul* she shows us the
wonderful way her prayers were answered, and how, out of
the pit of depression following her husband's death, she was
able to return to work as a teacher and use her experiences
and the companionship of friends to help others, realising
that "Christ is Lord both of Life and of Death".

It was Fr. Huw Ballard Thomas who once pointed out that
"God never closes a door without opening a window". He said
that if we stop struggling by our own strength and surrender
ourselves to Christ, then we discover the presence of God
pouring out His love and power in and through the darkness.

This is exactly what Mrs. Urch has done, and how she was
enabled to do it she tells us in this little book.

STUART HIBBERD

Contents

BE STILL, MY SOUL

Be still, my soul: the Lord is on thy side;
   Bear patiently the cross of grief and pain;
Leave to thy God to order and provide;
   In every change He faithful will remain.
Be still, my soul: thy best, thy heavenly Friend
Through thorny ways leads to a joyful end.

Be still, my soul: thy God doth undertake
   To guide the future as He has the past.
Thy hope, Thy confidence let nothing shake;
   All now mysterious shall be bright at last.
Be still, my soul: the winds and waves still know
His voice Who ruled them while He dwelt below.

Be still, my soul: when dearest friends depart,
   And all is darkened in the vale of tears,
Then shalt thou better know His love, His heart,
   Who comes to soothe thy sorrow and thy fears.
Be still, my soul: thy Jesus can repay,
From His own fulness, all He takes away.

Be still, my soul: the hour is hastening on
   When we shall be forever with the Lord,
Where disappointment, grief and fear are gone,
   Sorrow forgot, love's purest joys restored.
Be still, my soul: when change and tears are past,
All safe and blessed we shall meet at last.

KATHARINA VON SCHLEGEL, 1697–?
translated by
JANE LAURIE BORTHWICK, 1813–97

Thorny Ways

ONE CALM BRIGHT EVENING during the summer in which I was thirty-five years old, I was sitting in a seaside church in the North of Ireland. We were on holiday, and at the guest house where we were staying our three children were sound asleep. Michael, our eldest, was almost thirteen. Maureen was just past her ninth birthday, and Rosalind was six.

I was feeling particularly happy and relaxed that evening. For one thing, *all* our three children were on holiday with us. Just recently we had welcomed Michael back into our home after a grave illness. Also Walter, my husband, was beside me in the pew instead of occupying his usual place in the pulpit. I think only a Manse wife can appreciate the peculiar holiday joy which envelops the members of a Manse family when they sit in a strange pew, listening to a good sermon from a preacher with whom they are not intimately involved emotionally, or for whom they are not personally responsible.

The sermon that summer evening was impressive. It was entitled "Life's Cruel Sea". The minister spoke of the mystery of pain and death, human suffering and loss. After the address we sang the moving hymn,

> *Be still, my soul: the Lord is on thy side;*

to the equally moving tune *Finlandia* by Sibelius.

For both Walter and myself there seemed to be a significance in every word, and the memory of the service, its message and its atmosphere, seemed afterwards preternaturally sharp. We talked about our impressions as we walked along the seashore on our way home to the children, and we both agreed the service had been particularly meaningful because of the recent months of anxiety from which we had only just emerged.

I have touched very briefly on this anxiety in my previous book *Queen of the Manse*,[1] which I wrote under the pen name of Elise Brogan. Michael, a fine sturdy lad of twelve, had wakened up one morning near Christmas with a temperature of 105°. We could not remember him having been sick since he had had measles six years earlier. Just two days previous to his high temperature he had played an energetic game of rugger, so though he seemed very ill we were not unduly worried. But in the days that followed he lost weight rapidly, and it was not long before we knew he had tuberculosis, and would have to face several months bedfast.

The shock and disappointment were severe for us all. He had just completed his first term at High School. We wondered what the future held for him. But gradually we all adjusted ourselves to the new situation, and proved the truth of the words,

> *Faith came singing into the room*
> *And the other guests took flight.*
> *Grief and anxiety, fear and gloom*
> *Fled out into the night.*
> *And I wondered that such peace could be,*
> *But Faith said gently, "Don't you see,*
> *They cannot live with me?"* [2]

[1] *Queen of the Manse,* Elizabeth Urch's first book to which several references are made, is regrettably out of print.
[2] At present I am unable to trace the source of this verse, but shall make due acknowledgment in later editions when the source is known.

The months of Michael's illness had seemed unduly long, but now he was convalescent, and the main anxiety was over. As we walked the seashore that calm, windless night, we were enveloped in peace. We felt sure that we were nearing the "joyful end" mentioned in the hymn we had just sung, after having been led along thorny paths.

Michael went back to school that autumn after we returned to Scotland. During the months of the winter which followed, my husband and I would often recall the feelings we had both experienced in that Irish seaside church. It was not long before we realised why God had spoken so forcibly to us, especially in the words,

> Be still, my soul: the Lord is on thy side;
> Bear patiently the cross of grief and pain;
> Leave to thy God to order and provide;
> In every change He faithful will remain.
> Be still, my soul: thy best, thy heavenly Friend,
> Through thorny ways leads to a joyful end.

Walter was of fine, stalwart physique—a handsome and imposing figure. He was rarely ill and seemed to have an insatiable desire for study and hard work. During the winter which followed our Irish holiday he not only fulfilled all his own congregational duties, but he also undertook many outside preaching engagements. He prepared and delivered lectures to students; he spent long hours on some thoughtful lectures on "Ethics" for the local trainee Marriage Guidance Counsellors; he examined theses submitted by young probationer ministers.

As the summer approached I felt that he was becoming over-tired, and I was looking forward to the holidays so that he could enjoy a much-needed break. Just as our leave was

about to start he collapsed in a strange pulpit while conduct-
ing a service for a colleague. The doctors felt sure, as I did,
that he had been over-working. We all believed that a few
weeks' rest and quiet would fit him again for his arduous
duties.

But, as the days stretched into weeks, there was, instead of
improvement, a disturbing deterioration. He was rarely free
from agonising, prostrating headaches. I tried to withhold
my growing anxiety from him and the children, but one day
I was so over-wrought that I broke down by his bedside and
wept. He took me in his arms and said, "I have been through
some anxious days too. But I want you to believe what is
now my own firm conviction. The Lord is going to take care
of me, and He's going to take care of you, and of our
children."

Together we recalled the Irish service of the previous year.
Could it really be only twelve months since we had been so
enveloped in peace? Recent weeks of anxiety and pain had
seemed like months in themselves. So this was why God had
written so indelibly on our memories the message of that
previous year's sermon, "Life's Cruel Sea".

I sat down by Walter's bedside, and quietly sang again the
lines, "Be still, my soul". It was in those words that we found
strength in the days which followed when his condition
deteriorated so rapidly that he had to be rushed eighty miles
to another city to consult a neuro-surgeon. It was not long
before I knew that he had a malignant brain tumour; that
the outlook was extremely grave; that, even if he recovered
physically for a time, there was scant hope of him ever
returning to his duties as a minister.

I was shattered. Life for us had seemed to be at its fullest
and happiest. Could it be that it was all to end so tragically,
so soon? By the time the day of the major operation arrived

I had tried to convince myself that the prospect might not be really as bad as the surgeon feared. Maybe the tumour would not prove to be malignant. Perhaps this experience was just another thorny way, like Michael's illness, and the joyful end would come when I saw the surgeon after the operation. Maybe he would say, "Your husband will be all right."

But when I saw him he did not say, "Your husband will be all right." He said instead, "He may live for three months. He may live for eighteen. But for all practical purposes you ought to reconcile yourself to the sad fact that his active life as a minister is over. You have three children. Go home to them now and make your plans."

The surgeon spoke in a restrained and sympathetic voice. I was stunned. Though still I repeated over and over to my-self the words, "Be still, my soul: the Lord is on thy side", yet there was one verse which I could not really believe would apply to me.

> *Be still, my soul: when dearest friends depart,*
> *And all is darkened in the vale of tears,*
> *Then shalt thou better know His love, His heart,*
> *Who comes to soothe thy sorrow and thy fears.*
> *Be still, my soul: thy Jesus can repay,*
> *From His own fulness, all He takes away.*

I went home to our children, and I began days of searching, earnest argument with God. I had always believed in God's power to heal. Now I *demanded* healing of God as if it were mine by right. My husband was a useful man. God knew how many had been influenced over the years by his quiet wisdom, his deep humility, his clear courage, his transparent honesty. "The straightest man we ever knew," was how someone described him to me at this time. Defiantly I asked God, "Is such a life just to be snuffed out? Surely you have some better, some higher thing in store for us than just this?"

Often when we watch intense suffering we try to seek some new, some satisfying answer to the problem of pain. I have never really found a complete answer. I only know that it was through watching Walter in terrible agony that I eventually came to the place of complete submission to the will of God.

There was a steady and rapid deterioration in his condition in the weeks following the operation. He could not speak clearly, and he was quite unable to read or write. The area of his brain controlling these functions was damaged, it seemed, beyond repair. We both believed in God's power to heal; so did our church members, and many, many praying friends. They prayed unceasingly for his recovery.

As the days passed, however, and I sat by his bedside watching his increasing pain, and the continual deterioration in his mental abilities, I got quite beyond struggling in prayer with God about healing. I was quite beyond asking any longer for recovery. All I asked was that Walter should be released from his sufferings which already had been too great.

After returning one day from the hospital, I flung myself down in desperation upon my knees by my bedside "clean forspent". My surrender was complete. For the first time I told God that if it were His will to take my husband to Himself, then in willingness I would give him up. I would fully trust Him to care for myself and the children. I would believe that He would help me to bring them up without the strong support I had always enjoyed from a loved partner. For many days previously, when I had knelt to pray for healing, there had often come to me Christ's question, "Lovest thou Me more than these?" Now, for the first time, I felt that I could answer truthfully, "Yes." All bitterness and protest were gone, and I felt that God had swept my own self-will up into His own higher and better will.

I had been through my Gethsemane, and though much sorrow was still to come, yet the main battle was won. I had gone into the woods "clean forspent"; I came out "well content".

> *Into the woods my Master went,*
> *Clean forspent, forspent.*
> *Into the woods my Master came,*
> *Forspent with love and shame.*
> *But the olives were not blind to Him:*
> *The little grey leaves were kind to Him,*
> *The thorn tree had a mind to Him*
> *When into the woods He came.*
>
> *Out of the woods my Master went,*
> *And He was well content.*
> *Out of the woods my Master came,*
> *Content with death and shame.*
> *When Death and Shame would woo Him last,*
> *From under the trees they drew Him last;*
> *'Twas on a tree they slew Him last*
> *When out of the woods He came.*
>
> SIDNEY LANIER (1)

I was once more enveloped in peace. I did not doubt God's power to heal Walter if He still willed it, but I was able to say something like the three Hebrew boys in Daniel, "Our God is able to deliver; but if He chooses not to, yet I will trust Him."

The days following were different. Where previously I had been tearful and ill-composed, now I was able, with God's help, to maintain an inner and outer calm. My thoughts generally became less confused and rebellious.

It is only when we come to care more about God and His will than about our own destiny and happiness that character can be transformed, and our destiny shaped aright. Once we reach the place of transferring our whole attention from self, or even from those we love, to God and His will, only then do we find the secret of real peace and serenity. There comes then the deepest assurance that our interests are safer than we can ever imagine when they are put into the hands of God. I knew beyond doubt that afternoon of surrender that whatever God's plan was for us all, even if it meant losing the one we loved so much, it would be far better than anything I could plan or desire in health, happiness or security.

2

A Moment of Truth

I⟀ was a few weeks after the operation. Walter was now in a hospital near our home. Although he could not speak clearly, I always seemed to know what he was trying to say, and I was sure that one of his dearest wishes was to be back in his own home. The inevitable hospital noises meant for him agonising pain. Even a small necessary light left on in the ward caused a searing torment in his eyes, and I knew that his inability to say what he wanted was perhaps the greatest trial of all.

So I decided to bring him home. I was warned that this might mean twenty-four-hour nursing on my part. There were those who felt that by having such a sick person in the house I should be subjecting my children to unnecessary strain. But there are a few times in life—only a few, I think— when we know beyond doubt that a decision we have to make is absolutely correct. For me this was one such occasion.

So we brought Walter home, as we thought, to weeks of waiting and watching for his death. My children, however, never ceased to pray for his restoration, and I found that young though they were they had an immensely deep and compassionate understanding of suffering. I believe this experience has given them a lasting gentleness towards those in pain or distress. Tenderness is a virtue often born out of sorrow. The hard and bitter experiences of our own lives create in us a power to feel for and help others.

Boisterous though the children normally were, now, without having to be told, they opened and shut doors gently and spoke quietly, though not always solemnly.

Our youngest child, Rosalind, was just seven, and day by day she brought her school reading book to her Daddy, to try to teach him how to read again. From time to time each one of the children would, quite naturally and without prompting, sit down beside him and try to help him to repeat their names, for when he returned from hospital he was quite unable to call his own children by name. Each day they would bring pencil and paper to him to try to show him how to write again.

What should we do when we realise that someone we love very dearly has only a short time to live? Should we hold the information tenaciously to ourselves? Should we try to make the patient believe he is improving day by day when we know in fact that, medically speaking, there is no hope? Or should we tell him the truth?

Some time or other, most of us will have to face this problem, and it is difficult. But it becomes less difficult if we can manage to put things in their true perspective. Life and healing for so many of us seem to be the most important things of all. Yet salvation and a right relationship with God are of far greater importance. Once we realise the greatness of this truth we become less rebellious about sickness and bereavement. Death does not break our fellowship with God. Dying does not mean going out into the dark. If our trust is in Christ, it means going out to be with Him.

This is something tremendous to hold on to when we wrestle with the problem, Should our loved ones be told the truth? Of course the basis for such a disclosure should lie much further back in life. We should have such a close fellowship with those we love, such an intimate spiritual communion, that when it comes to matters of life and death we should not be completely inarticulate.

I think it was while pondering this question that I became so sure it was right for me to bring Walter home. I knew that on several occasions he was wishing me to speak to him fully about his condition, but it was obvious that the public hospital ward was not the place for me to talk of such matters. I knew also about the division of medical opinion on this great question. Many doctors feel that to tell a person he is about to die is bound to have a grave mental and psychological effect on him. They feel no one should be deprived of all hope, even though, medically speaking, there is no hope. They fear an uncontrollable reaction.

I knew all these arguments, but I also knew my husband. I knew his faith, and I knew his intelligence. He was far too wise a man not to understand the seriousness of his condition, sooner or later. Also, I have always believed that uncertainty is harder to bear than the truth, however harsh. But over and above all these reasons there was the main one that during all our married life we had always sought to be frank and truthful with each other. I could not bear to think that during our last days together there might arise a barrier of deceit and lies, when I should have to pretend he was getting well again, knowing only too well that he was not. It would have been completely intolerable for me to try to maintain an untruth. Such a barrier would have been too hard for me to bear. So my husband had to be told. I would not entertain a "conspiracy of silence".

In his presidential address to the Manchester Medical Society on October 31st, 1962, Sir Robert Platt spoke clearly about this "conspiracy of silence". He said:

"A conspiracy of silence usually surrounds the whole question of death, a silence as much due to the patient's avoidance of the subject as the doctor's. Patients do not frequently seek to have their worst fears confirmed, and some I am sure are unwilling to put their doctors into an embarrassing position. . . .

"I have no doubt at all that most patients faced with dangerous or mortal illness recognise their danger, if their mind is clear, though few regard death as inevitable. The occasions are rare when a discussion on death, at the bedside, is appropriate; but I think more opportunity should be given for such discussions if the patient indicates a wish for them. Far too often he falls into the mutual conspiracy of silence, for if his first approaches are met with an immediate rebuff by the doctor who brushes aside all likelihood of a fatal outcome, the patient is not encouraged to express his fears or discuss his feelings. He keeps them privately to himself, but the doctor is mistaken if he thinks his superficial assurances are accepted. He has merely given the patient the impression that the voicing of his most precious thoughts and fears will be unwelcome."(2)

Walter and I were fortunate in having as our family doctor one who was understanding, and who now accepted my point of view. Together we reached the decision that when the opportune moment arrived one or other of us would tell Walter the truth. This was not something to be blurted out tearfully and clumsily on my part. I had to pray much that if I were to be the one to speak, then I might recognise the proper moment and be given the right words.

In *Queen of the Manse* I had written about preparing people for death because we had come up against it so often in our congregational duties. I wrote of an instance known to us then—an instance which I believe prepared me for the difficult moment when it came in my own home. I quote from my chapter "Crossing the Bar".

"In one of our hospitals was a patient in his middle forties—dying, and he knew it. Though he had enjoyed a good deal of prosperity in his life, he had unfortunately left God out of it. Indeed, he had gone so far as to leave instructions in his will that no service was to be conducted for him when he died, as he was an unbeliever. In the closing weeks of his life his attitude changed a little, and one day, when a parson looked into his ward, he gruffly asked, 'Can you tell a bloke how to die?' The parson, God forgive him, talked about the weather!"

At the time I wrote these words I was greatly concerned, as was my husband, about the complete inability which exists in many people, even in trained clergy, to speak about matters of the very highest importance. I believed then, as I believed throughout our own sorrow, that it is wrong for any person to be allowed to make the journey into the Great Beyond without being helped to make some personal preparation.

It is, I think, helpful when we ponder this great subject to study what was our Lord's attitude to death, and especially to His own death. He certainly did not try to hide His coming sorrow from His disciples. In fact, He talked freely about it, and warned them of what was going to happen to Him in Jerusalem. But He never spoke of His death alone. He spoke always of His triumph over death, and of His Resurrection from the dead. His death was only one episode in a series of mighty acts by which God's glory was to be revealed. His preparation was not only for Good Friday, but also for Holy Saturday, Easter Day and Pentecost.

This is a guide to us. I am sure of this—if we are to tell a person that he is going to die, then we must also point him, through our Lord Jesus Christ, to the hope that is ours beyond the grave. Christ is the only One I know Who can give the strength and serenity needed to face the journey into the unknown.

So it was that I told Walter myself about his condition during the quiet of an evening when he was enjoying one of his brief respites from pain. He had been becoming progressively weaker, and his sufferings greater, in the few days since his return from hospital, and I felt that we were not to be together very much longer. While talking to him I tried, with God's help, to strike a balance between the constant upsurge of foolish hope and the cold extinction of all hope. With the talk many tensions were released, and the last barrier was down between us. I felt sure that we should be able to give each other strength in the dark days ahead.

It would be wrong for me to try to suggest that there was no sadness that evening. I knew Walter was not afraid of death, but he was sorrowful at the thought of leaving us all. I knew he longed to be able to see his children grow up. I knew he realised something of the burden I would have to face. But there was a serenity in our sadness because we were both confident that God would guide the future as He had the past. I am very glad now that I told him.

Just after our conversation finished I could see that he was wearied and weak, so I made him comfortable and he fell into what seemed to be the first natural, undrugged sleep for weeks. Our doctor was very attentive, coming in several times daily to give injections which would ease the agonising pain and induce sleep. His last visit each day was around 11 p.m. When he came in this momentous evening, he stood by Walter's bedside, needle poised ready to give the injection which would give us a quiet night's rest. I said to him, "Walter has been sleeping deeply since early evening. Isn't that very unusual just at this time before the injection?"

He then examined Walter fully, put the needle away, and said, without explanation, "I do not think he will need this tonight." I was slightly uneasy in case Walter should wake

26

later with pain which I would not be able to control. But the doctor left me a drug which could, if necessary, be given orally. He said he would return in the morning as usual.

When dawn broke Walter woke up, refreshed as I had not seen him for many weeks, and without pain. His first words that morning were, "Darling, I am not going to die yet. God has still some work for me to do." I just stared at him in amazement before rushing to him, overcome. He was speaking clearly. He was free from pain. This was the first time since his operation that I had seen him thus. He got out of bed there and then and walked unaided about the room. When I offered help, he smilingly put me aside.

When the children came in before school he was sitting in a chair, and he called them each by name, clearly and distinctly. They were overjoyed! So was the doctor when he arrived a little later, and saw him and listened to him, alert and articulate for the first time for many weeks.

A few days later my husband conducted family prayers with myself and the children, and he wrote his first short letter to a loved aunt who he knew had been bearing his sorrow with him. He went out into the garden, and talked quite freely and naturally with friends and neighbours. Everyone was astounded.

Just prior to the quiet of that evening when we had spoken together of the gravity of his illness a ministerial colleague had come to see him. Only a very few close friends were allowed to see him at that period, and then only very briefly. All the blinds were drawn that afternoon as Walter was still suffering excruciating torment in his eyes from light and colour. Reluctantly we had to remove a most beautiful bowl of flowers, which had just been placed in his bedroom, as the brilliance of the blooms caused a fiery agony when his eyes caught them. Our friend tiptoed quietly to the bedside, and said a very short and quiet prayer. I knew from his demeanour that he felt it might well be the last he would say with my husband, for his weakening state was very obvious.

Four days later he tiptoed to the room again. The flowers were back in place, and when I said, "You will find Walter in the garden," his mouth just fell open in astonishment, and he stared at me in disbelief. I led him out to where Walter was enjoying the autumn sunshine. Gently he placed his hand on my husband's shoulder, and said, shaking his head, "Walter, we have all been praying for this remarkable recovery. Now that it has come we are unprepared for it. O ye of little faith!"

The Biblical saints, Walter reminded us, were little better than ourselves. We talked of the prayer meeting in Jerusalem held after the imprisonment of the Apostle Peter (Acts 12: 12). No doubt the company gathered in prayer in the house of Mary, the mother of John Mark, were earnestly beseeching God for Peter's release. Yet when he appeared at their door, and Rhoda ran in and reported his coming, their only retort was, "You must be mad!"

3

Miles to Go

THERE WAS A LUXURY in our togetherness in the days following the remarkable recovery, which was all the more en-
joyable because we discovered that my husband's natural
gaiety and sense of humour had not been impaired by his
severe illness.

As soon as he could speak clearly, and was out of bed, he
asked the doctor if he could have a bath—a real bath, not
one of those blanket things he had had for weeks. The doctor
came into the room just after Walter returned from enjoying
the luxury, and his greeting was, "Well, how do you feel
after your first bath?" "Decidedly cleaner!" was the quick
retort, so much in contrast to the fumbling, agonising speech
of a day or so before that I saw the doctor's eyebrows rise
in pleased surprise as he joined in the happy laughter.

We had many such happy moments in which our children
joined, and it was wonderful to hear the house ring again
with jollity and merriment. We did not talk much now about
the far-distant future. We were content for the moment
that God had given us this time together. Each day we
thanked Him for health and sanity of mind. We both knew
that the tumour had been malignant, and that complete
healing was something which could not be claimed at this
early stage. But constantly we thanked God for a remarkable

recovery, and with His help we tried to live one day at a time, leaving the future in God's hands.

Every moment with each other was precious as never before, but it was not for this alone that Walter believed he had been restored. He became urgent in his requests to be allowed to return to some of his duties. He did not have the complete physical strength necessary to cope with all the duties of the ministry, but he was sure that God had restored him in order to use him, and he was eager to be back in harness.

Less than a month after his return from hospital he attended church, and he spoke a few deeply-moving sentences of thanks to his people, and led them in prayer. Immediately after this service he set about preparing a sermon which he preached a fortnight later.

The sermon he had last preached, just before becoming ill, was on the text, "Woe is me, if I preach not the Gospel." This text was very clearly in my mind now as I saw his desire and strong determination to preach again. I knew that for him life would be a barren thing if he could not proclaim the Gospel of Christ. We would sometimes think of Robert Frost's words from *Stopping By Woods On A Snowy Evening*.

> *The woods are lovely, dark and deep,*
> *But I have promises to keep,*
> *And miles to go before I sleep."* (3)

My husband seemed to be aware constantly of promises he must fulfil, and miles still to travel—with perhaps not too long a time left for the fulfilment and the travelling.

During this period of recovery he was, of course, able to receive many more visitors than during his weeks of great suffering. There was one thing above all else about these visits which seemed to impress him—or, rather, depress him. It was the number of people who said to him, "We cannot understand why this should have been allowed to happen to you—you of all people!"

He was not flattered by such remarks. He told me that they merely indicated that he had failed somewhere in his ministry to these people. "I have somehow," he said, "not made it clear to them that the Christian must never expect to be immune from sorrow and suffering; that God has no favourites; that He owes us nothing in health or happiness or prosperity."

That was why, when he chose the text for his first sermon following his illness, it was 1 Peter 4: 12, 13: "Beloved, think it not strange concerning the fiery trial which is to try you, as though some strange thing happened unto you; but rejoice, inasmuch as ye are partakers of Christ's sufferings; that when his glory shall be revealed, ye may be glad also with exceeding joy."

I quote his sermon verbatim.

"A few weeks ago the doctors were of the opinion that it would be many, many months before I was able to undertake my work again, and there was the grave possibility that I would never be able to do so. But here in this church you lovingly prayed for me. And throughout this city Christians of all denominations met and prayed for me. And during my illness ministers of all denominations visited me. And prayed with me. More than that, throughout all the country, there has gone up a great volume of loving and persistent prayer. God heard and answered, and humbly I say, 'Here I am today, to minister the Word of God to you once again.'

"The text I want to bring you is this one which comes from 1 Peter 4: 12, 13.

"I want you to think first of all of Christ's suffering. He

hangs upon that cruel cross, His pale body besmeared with blood from wounds made by thorns and nails and spear. The wooden cross and the rough earth around are drenched with the precious blood of our dying Lord.

"Now He is dead. Down this hill called Calvary moves a stream of Pharisees and priests, outwardly gloating and inwardly satisfied. Listen with me to their conversation:

" 'Well, gentlemen, He is finished now, and will soon be forgotten. We are successful at last. He has been proved a failure.'

" 'Yes, you are right. His influence is finished now for ever.'

" 'His triumph was short-lived. We are the victors. We have disgraced Him upon that cross, and all the country will despise Him for ever.'

"Suppose we could raise those Pharisees and their wicked associates from the dead this Sunday morning. Suppose we could take them to the multitude of buildings throughout the world that we call churches and chapels. Suppose we could ask them to listen to the hymns of praise and worship ascending to that same Man of Calvary. Whom would they regard as triumphant now?

> *In the Cross of Christ I glory,*
> *Towering o'er the wrecks of time,*
> *All the light of sacred story*
> *Gathers round His head sublime.*

"How unspeakably mystified and rebuked His enemies would be! *Suffering led to salvation, and trials led to triumph.*

"In our text Peter associated our Lord and His sufferings with the sufferings of all who are His followers. And Peter was not the only Apostle who wrote in this way. Paul was constantly making the same association. He talked not only of the 'consolation' of Christ abounding in us, but also of 'the sufferings' of Christ abounding in us.

"Let us go in thought now to the jail at Philippi. Outside the jail is a crowd of jeering, mocking persecutors. Let us listen to them talking.

" 'Well, we've got Paul now. And we'll finish him now that we have got him.'

" 'You are right. His influence is destroyed for ever.'

"Had they been able to hear the voice of the Almighty that day, they might have heard Him say,

" 'You are *not* right. *You* have not got Paul. *I* have got him. His influence is not destroyed for ever.'

"The enemies of Paul did not hear the Almighty's voice, but Paul and Silas did. And at midnight they could both pray to Him, and sing His praises. What happened? Why, the other prisoners heard them, and later, after the earthquake, the jailer came and found Christ. His family came and found Christ too, and the first seeds of the church at Philippi were sown. *Sorrow again turned to a song, and afflictions turned to triumph.*

"Let us leave the scene at Philippi now. Come with me to watch another scene. A little ship is approaching the shores of a small island. The men on board are prisoners—rough, brazen, blasphemous, uncouth. But among them is an old man—gentle, holy, refined, and handsome of countenance. What a tragedy, you say, that such a man as John should be cast away among such company, upon such an island as Patmos. But read what he wrote when he was on that island —the book of Revelation.

" 'I was in the Spirit on the Lord's day . . .'

"He saw the Lord in all His glory. He saw, too, that those ruled by Satan and sin were like wild, ravenous beasts, and

33

much of his writing paints a dark and terrible picture. But he does not end there. He takes us on to see the triumph of God and of our Lord over all that is dark and sinful. In the end, we see the Holy City, the New Jerusalem, and we hear the *new* song. Did John resent going to Patmos? Did he say, 'Why has all this happened to me?' I think not.

"But let us not stop at linking the sufferings of our Lord, and the sufferings of His followers, only with those whose names are written in the pages of Scripture. History is also full of the names of those who have sorrowed and triumphed; who have turned seeming defeat into victory.

"If you knew that tomorrow you would be burnt to death, do you think that tonight you could sleep peaceably? It was the evening before Bishop Ridley was to be burnt at the stake in Oxford, in 1555. His brother was with him on that last evening, and offered to remain and watch all night with him.

" 'No, no,' replied the bishop. 'That you shall not. For I mind, God willing, to go to bed, and to sleep as quietly tonight as I ever did in my life.'

"In the morning he was taken to the fire, and he did die. But his influence and his triumphant spirit have lived everlastingly.

"From my study window I can get a glimpse of the historical city of St. Andrews. Outside the university there you can see in the road a circle of stones, and within the circle the initials P.H. If you go farther down to the castle, you can see a similar circle, and within it the initials G.W. Those circles mark the spots where Patrick Hamilton and George Wishart allowed themselves to be burnt rather than deny the Lord they both loved. They were men of gentle nature and loving hearts. Can you say that the death of such men at the hands of such cruel, callous executioners was defeat? Surely not, for men who saw them die, in supernal glory, found through their death the way of life. And throughout all the years since, their sufferings have been an influence for righteousness and truth.

"I move over the centuries now to a man nearer our own time and age—a man who laboured for a quarter of a century in missionary work in Mongolia. He died without seeing one Mongolian convert baptised. James Gilmour, for the sake of Christ, suffered terrible bodily discomfort and pain, intense loneliness and opposition. No doubt the greatest suffering of all was to see no fruit for his labour. Yet who will say that James Gilmour was a failure when his life speaks so eloquently to posterity.

"But, you might say, these are exceptional people—people of extraordinary stature and strength. Yet, in ordinary circles, there have been, and are, multitudes who have been willing to be partakers in Christ's sufferings. Granted there are many who grumble and resent every trial. There are all too many who say, 'Why has this happened to me?' as though in some way or other God owed it to them to keep them perpetually free from suffering and affliction. God has never promised any of us freedom from pain, trials or distresses. To expect such a freedom is a sign of an immature faith, and a lack of knowledge and understanding of the Scriptures. 'Beloved, think it not strange concerning the fiery trial. . . .'

"At our family worship the other day I read from the little magazine *The Upper Room* the story of a young girl called Beulah who trained to be a nurse. She had just embarked on her career when she was stricken with arthritis. No doubt many questioned the Lord's dealings, and the reason for Beulah's sufferings. But not Beulah. She had a special telephone installed by her bedside, and daily she used it to inspire her friends, to encourage members of her church, to comfort the bereaved, and to bring cheer to the discouraged. At the age of thirty-six she died. Was the life of this young woman, crippled as she was, a life of defeat? Was her early death a tragedy? How can it be when her influence for good was felt so strongly by those who knew her? How can it be when today, through the medium of *The Upper Room*, her whole story and influence have spread to many countries of the world to people who never knew her?

"You who are listening to me here this morning have had, and will have, your own individual trials and testings. 'Think it not strange. . . .'

"It is how we react to our sufferings which determines whether they will be turned into triumph or defeat. There is nothing in ourselves which can determine victory, but it is as we draw upon Christ's grace that we shall be sure of ultimate triumph. The testimony of Paul, of John, of Bishop Ridley, of Patrick Hamilton, of George Wishart, of James Gilmour of Mongolia, would be, 'His grace is sufficient for me.'

"If in such circumstances of extreme testing and trial these men could so display faith and courage and joy, cannot we, with our lesser trials and testings, do just that?

"The text we have used speaks of trials and sufferings, but note what Peter says: '*Rejoice.*' That is it. And the last words of the text are '*exceeding joy*'. God grant that by allowing ourselves to be partakers in Christ's sufferings, when His glory shall be revealed, we may be glad also with exceeding joy."

*   *   *   *

It was just nine weeks since the brain operation, and this moving and meaningful sermon was delivered with great power. He did not falter for a word. We were all filled with awed praise, and as we stood to sing the hymn he had chosen to follow the sermon, we felt we realised with deeper insight than ever before what the hymn writer, F. W. Faber, meant in his words of worship and commitment. We sang the hymn to the well-known tune of Lloyd. I have rarely heard a hymn sung with deeper reverence and devotion.

> *I worship Thee, sweet will of God!*
> *And all Thy ways adore;*
> *And every day I live I long*
> *To love Thee more and more.*
>
> *I have no cares, O blessed Will!*
> *For all my cares are Thine;*
> *I live in triumph, Lord, for Thou*
> *Hast made Thy triumphs mine.*
>
> *Ride on, ride on, triumphantly,*
> *Thou glorious Will, ride on.*
> *Faith's pilgrim sons behind Thee take*
> *The road that Thou hast gone.*
>
> *He always wins who sides with God,*
> *To him no chance is lost;*
> *God's will is sweetest to him when*
> *It triumphs at his cost.*
>
> *Ill that He blesses is our good,*
> *And unblest good is ill;*
> *And all is right that seems most wrong,*
> *If it be His sweet will.*

My husband was well known in the city where he minis-tered, and the Press did not fail to see in the usual church notices that he was billed to speak that Sunday morning. They telephoned him afterwards, and asked for an interview and a picture.

He always loathed sensationalism, and he was afraid of distortion and extravagant claims which he knew would do more harm than good. So he talked the matter over first with his doctor who simply said, "There is no doubt from a medical point of view that your recovery is remarkable. Perhaps your story may keep someone from despair." It was with this attitude that he allowed himself to be interviewed.

At his request the journalists were restrained in their reports, and in simple, straightforward language they told the story of his recovery. There was no doubt that many were helped.

Just one thing worried him about the publicity. He said to me, "In all these reports—indeed, in my own sermon—it has been emphasised what a volume of prayer has ascended to God on my behalf. Many poor souls who read this story, or who have heard my words, are not blessed with a great number of sympathetic and loving friends such as I have. We must make it clear to them that God is the same God, whether the volume of prayer be great or small. If one of these needy people has but one person to pray for him—or even if there is no one but the sufferer himself to pray—still God is the same, and He can do the same again. The effectual fervent prayer of *one* righteous man availeth much."

Each Sunday after this my husband preached either morning or evening. He also sought to do a little of every type of duty which falls to a minister. He administered Communion. He wrote letters. He visited the sick. He comforted the bereaved. He periodically undertook to give the children's talk on Sunday mornings.

His natural compassion for the suffering and the bereaved

seemed to be much deeper now because of his own stern trial. When he prayed for people there was no doubt in anyone's mind that he was in truth entering into the experience of all sufferers, and bearing their burdens on his own heart.

He never entered the pulpit easily or glibly after his recovery. Perhaps I was the only one who knew what each sermon cost him in preparation and delivery. After all, his illness had begun with a collapse at the start of one such sermon. The memory of those awful moments never left him, and he knew that if once he focussed his mind on his own weakness, instead of the strength which God could provide, then there could be disaster again.

He had always a great gift for children's talks, and the adults in his congregation often felt they were helped as much by the junior sermon as by the adult one.

I was startled myself at times when I realised how keen his wit still was, despite the terrible injuries to his brain. Perhaps the wittiest of his talks was one to the children one Sunday morning shortly after his recovery.

He looked all round the company of boys and girls and then he confided to them, with a twinkle in his eyes and mock solemnity, "Do you know, children, we have a dreadful liar in our house!" There were quite a few surreptitious glances at the Manse children, two of whom had noticeably reddened, wondering what dreadful exposure was to be made.

Then he continued, "When it is twelve o'clock, this liar will sometimes tell us that it is only a quarter to twelve. Or when it's time for the six o'clock news, the liar will say, 'You needn't switch that radio on. You're too late. It's already a quarter-past six.'"

There was almost an audible sigh of relief as every one realised the only Manse liar to be publicly denounced was an old clock.

So he went on, saying that this timepiece had let us down so often that we had now ceased to believe it—even when it might be telling the truth.

Vividly he painted the picture, and just as vividly the children realised that if they were to grow up with the habit of lying there might come a day when they desperately wanted to be believed, and it would be too late. For people always cease to trust a persistent liar.

As we went back to the Manse we joked about the reactions of the family to the sermon. We went affectionately to the room where the clock rested on a shelf just to see if it were still telling lies. It had stopped completely! No amount of shaking, winding, cleaning, or poking would start it again. And in fact it has never gone since.

Well, of course, the next children's sermon was ready made. Walter began it by telling the children that he had never before realised that clocks had ears, and that they could understand human language. But not only had our clock heard his complaints the previous Sunday about its time-keeping, but it had there and then decided to act— well, just like so many boys and girls, and grown-ups he knew. It had turned huffy!

"What do you do, boys and girls, when someone decides to rebuke you about a fault you have? Do you go all sulky too, and refuse to speak or to help in any way at all? That's just what our clock has done!"

He went on to tell them that both now and later on in life they would be required to do jobs to help other people, both inside and outside the church. Some of these jobs they would do well, and some they would do badly. Often there would be criticism. What should be our correct attitude when people criticise what we do? Should we just down tools and say, "Well, if they don't like the way I'm doing it, let them go and find someone else"? Too many people in the world use this sulky way of dealing with criticism, he said. The better way is to find out how to rectify our mistakes, how to improve ourselves and our work so that we may offer ourselves more whole-heartedly in Christ's service, instead of withdrawing ourselves from it.

His mind worked clearly and efficiently during this period of convalescence. He was often physically tired, but he did not once rely on an old sermon—"ride an old horse", as he termed it. I think he was too grateful to be able to reason, to be able to read and write again, ever to consider rifling his "old sermon" box.

As Christmas came near there was fun and laughter in the house again, and Walter's ready wit entertained us on many occasions. One day I was shopping with him, and a very effusive woman was trying to convince us of the superlative value of some article we were inspecting. Every sentence was punctuated with the word "dear".

"Suits you beautifully, dear."

"A very good bargain, this, dear."

"You will not find better than this anywhere in the city, dear."

With firmness and obvious enjoyment he retorted, "No thank you, Madam. And may I say that the only *dear* thing about you is your produce."

4

The Vale of Tears

IT WAS just a year ago that my book *Queen of the Manse* had
been published. In it I had a chapter entitled "Crossing the
Bar" which I had then written with sincerity. Now I began
to wonder if it had not been effrontery for anyone whom
death had not brushed personally to try to write words of
comfort for others in distress. And yet the very writing of
that chapter proved to be a preparation for my own coming
sorrow. When the blow finally struck, I sat down and re-read
my own words in order to try to find comfort. We never
know when we write or speak how soon it may be necessary
to put to a personal test the theories and practices we have
recommended to others.

I had written such things as these:

"Spiritual joy is not at the mercy of men, or circumstances,
or even of death."

"Only those who are truly Christian can know the meaning
of that word 'Peace' in such circumstances as death."

"When I am face to face with deep and bitter tragedy, I
am more glad than I can ever express that 'God holds the
key of all unknown'."

"But even with that knowledge many funerals are difficult
for any minister to conduct, however deep his trust. What
man can escape the feeling of tragedy at the graveside . . .
of a young mother or father?"

"What minister does not know the utter futility of human speech when Death, stark and terrible, has stalked into a family circle, unexpectedly, and with merciless harshness?"

"A minister will only bring consolation through his own intercessory prayers, through bringing the sufferers face to face with Christ, Who came not to use any of His miraculous powers to banish pain and tragedy, but Who, through His own cruel death, entered into and fully shared our human lot. It is in such circumstances where the human heart is crying out for light that it is the minister's privilege and responsibility to give his flock the food necessary to stabilise their souls; to convey to them something of the eternal truth of Christ's invitation, even through suffering."

"I am convinced that it is not here that a man should try to solve insoluble problems—for the problem of suffering is in truth an insoluble one. . . . I have not yet heard any answer to the problem which satisfied a tortured, troubled heart and mind. I am convinced, anyway, that the response of a heart in agony is not to any intellectual argument, however clever, but to a person—and what person is adequate but the Person of our Loving Saviour? Only by trying to convey to the sufferers and the bereaved that God is not aloof, but exceedingly near and full of care, can we hope to heal the hurt. It is in the midst of suffering that we realise the value of our Christianity which has as its very life a Man of Sorrows, crowned with thorns, nailed to a cruel tree; a Christ Who tasted death for every man. And here it is too that we realise the value of our Christianity which has as its very life, not only a Man of Sorrows, but a living, resurrected Lord."

*　　*　　*　　*

One day before Walter became ill—indeed it was even before Michael's long illness—the text for the Sunday evening sermon had been chosen. It was Philippians 4: 6, 7 (R.V.):

"In nothing be anxious; but in everything by prayer and supplication with thanksgiving let your requests be made known unto God.
And the peace of God, which passeth all understanding, shall guard your hearts and thoughts in Christ Jesus."

At that time any anxieties we had in our home were very minor ones. Our children were happy and healthy, and so were we. Personal tragedy had not yet touched our lives.

Just before the evening service Walter said to me, "I hope my people will not think it presumptuous of me to try to teach them what real trust in anxiety means. So many of them have great burdens to bear—sorrow, grief, crippling illness, terrible poverty. They could so easily say, 'What does he know of real anxiety?'" Then he went on, "But God knows I believe this message, and God grant that if ever we are called upon to bear any great trouble, I shall be enabled to practise what I preach."

We were to find very soon what a tremendous help it is to know and believe God's promises before the time comes to have to rely wholeheartedly upon them.

Occasionally, when Walter went to London he would record a short sermon for broadcasting purposes. Just a few weeks before he became ill he recorded one which was broadcast later. I was not able to hear it over the air, but I have to-day a tape-recording of that sermon which he had entitled —prophetically I feel—"What will you do when the props give way?"

He said, "Health often deteriorates with alarming suddenness. Riches can take wings and fly away. Friends and loved ones are removed from us. . . . If we are to survive the destruction of these props, if we are to endure to the end, then God must do something for us. . . ."

One by one our earthly props were knocked from under us, and the last one crumbled one day early in the New Year when suddenly the terrible pain returned. The doctor came again, and the surgeon who had operated travelled down almost immediately to our home. Walter had written to this surgeon the day after preaching the first sermon of his convalescence. Shortly after receiving this letter he visited our city, and there was no doubt that he shared fully in the joy we all felt at Walter's unexpected and rapid recovery.

This time, however, his face was sad. He said to me, "When I saw your husband some weeks ago I should have described him as a man without disease. I had hoped so much for you all that he would have had longer with you."

Walter was able to talk a little to the surgeon, and he asked him for a full and frank report. Without removing from us the last shred of hope, the frank report was given. Walter looked very sad, moved his hand in my direction, and said, "I had so hoped to see my children grow up—to share the burden of their upbringing."

After the surgeon left Walter got out of bed and sat in a chair, and he talked to me for a little while about my future, and that of the children. He asked me how I felt. I did not feel very happy, but I spoke to him of my trust in God, and our shared belief that any separation would be but for a while. Gently he took my face in his hands, and said, looking right into my eyes, "You are strong, darling. God keep you so—always."

In moments of weakness, when faith wavers, and doubts dismay, I recall those words of his which I believe were really a prayer. "God keep you so—always." Then I know that my strength is not dependent on myself, or on my feelings, but upon the Strong Refuge to Whom I was committed during that evening of sadness.

After our talk Walter rose from his chair, and in great weakness he walked with me through the house to the cupboard where he had placed several bowls of carefully-planted bulbs. The green shoots were just appearing. With my help he carried them through to the room where his bed had been since his return from hospital. He placed the bulbs at various vantage points around the room where, day by day, he would be able to watch the progress of the snowdrops. They were, I believe, for both of us, in the days to come—days of agony and distress—symbols of the life eternal. The tempests of the previous winter had robbed the plants of every bloom, of every leaf. Yet when there seemed nothing left but a bare and desolate little bulb, still carefully sealed up within that wizened, brown little scrap was the material of leaf and flower for a new season. The tempests of sorrow had stripped our lives bare, but we were certain now that the buds of celestial hope would burst forth into flower, and bloom again in a better land.

The children knew that their Daddy had not been feeling so well again, but with the optimism of youth they regarded it merely as a passing set-back. Over and over again I wrestled with the problem, "How can I tell my children, who have been so confident that God has been making their Daddy well again, that he is going to die?"

I remember, a few days after he became confined to bed, sitting silently by his side and praying over and over again in the quiet of my heart, "Lord, help me to be able to break it to them in the right way." I never needed to. The next morning our youngest child, Rosalind, came to me and said that she wanted to speak to me about a feeling she had had in bed the previous night. She said, "Mummy, Jesus wants my Daddy up in heaven." We wept together then, but part of my tears were tears of joy that God had relieved me of one of my great burdens—how to tell the children that their Daddy, the one they loved so much, was dying.

Later that day Walter woke up after a short sleep, and he signalled me to his bedside. He told me that he had been dreaming. "Does God still talk to people in dreams?" he asked. "Anyhow," he went on, pausing in weakness from time to time, "it is quite clear to me now that God wants to take me home. I had hoped to be with you for longer. But if it is God's will to take me, then I must be willing to go." He told me then how he had felt that there was still much work for him to do on earth. "I had hoped," he said, "to be useful in God's service for a much longer time. But perhaps He has some work for me to do in a better land." Then he asked me to tell some of his family, who were far away, that he did not wish them to have any bitterness that his recovery had been so brief. "Tell them," he said, "whatever is God's will is what is right and best for us. Nothing can be wrong in our lives if God is allowed to be Lord."

I told him of how Rosalind had just that morning said to me, "Jesus wants my Daddy up in heaven." He smiled radiantly and whispered, "That is lovely." A moment or two later he said, as if pondering what his seven-year-old had said, "Perhaps in later years my children will be able to take up some of the work I am having to lay down."

There followed days of intense pain, and his speech and other faculties deteriorated rapidly. Yet the strange thing was that when he wanted to pray, or when he wanted to tell any of us that he loved us, the words were always there, clear and distinct. I remember how, one day, a distant friend associated with a college in which we were very interested tiptoed into the room. For several days Walter had been unable to speak, and he had indicated most of his needs by gesture. But when he opened his eyes and saw his friend he raised himself with unbelievable strength to a sitting position, and with a familiar gesture lifted his hand, indicating that he wished us to pray. Clearly and forcibly he prayed, and especially for the students in whom he was so interested.

I had never watched anyone die before, and I had wondered many times how I could see someone I loved go from me without my inner spirit crumbling. But always with the urge to give way, there would come too the urge to pray. And during prayer I experienced those moments which can never be proved by reasoning or argument—moments of intense awareness of the Power of the Presence of the Living Christ. It was then that I found the true meaning of the Biblical word *Comfort, con fort*—with strength. And I knew then the full meaning of "underneath are the Everlasting Arms".

Walter's last words, less than forty-eight hours before he died, were to his children. He enfolded each of them in his arms and said, "God bless you," and told them each that he loved them. Again it was my seven-year-old who put into words the restrained beauty and pathos of the moment. "Mummy," she said, "my Daddy has forgotten a lot of things since he took ill. But he still remembers the most wonderful things—all about God; and that he loves us." At that moment there came to me the words of our Lord telling us not to fear those that kill the body. It is only the things which kill the soul that are to be feared. Through my grief I saw the silver lining. This vile disease which was wasting and destroying my husband's fine earthly body had no power to destroy his soul and spirit. Love still continued. His worship of God still continued. The real personality within that wasting earthly body would live on, and we would meet again.

As I watched Walter die some hours later, there came vividly to my mind words which I had included in *Queen of the Manse*, and which I had often used to comfort other bereaved:

> *All which I took from thee I did but take,*
> *Not for thy harms,*
> *But just that thou might'st seek it in My arms.*
> *All that thy child's mistake*
> *Fancies as lost, I have stored for thee at home:*
> *Rise, clasp My hand and come!*[1]

I knew then that I must not wallow in the morass of grief and self-pity. I must rise, clasp His hand, and go forth, sure that when change and tears are forever past we should meet again, sorrows would be all forgotten, and Love's purest joys restored.

[1] Francis Thompson's *The Hound of Heaven.*

5

Children and Bereavement

THERE HAS always been a tendency to shut children out
from the two great mysteries—birth and death. We have,
in the past generation or so, made some efforts to rectify
our mistakes where the great mystery of birth is concerned.
We no longer talk about storks or gooseberry bushes. We try
to be frank with our children when they ask us questions
about birth. But we are still very reluctant to talk to them
about the other great mystery—death.

Some children, though not many, do not feel the need to
question because death has never brushed them personally.
There are others, like my own, whose questions are many
because they have lost a person they have loved beyond
measure. How can anyone explain to a child the meaning
of death? How can we help him to accept such a loss, and
bear it without bitterness?

It is true, I am sure, that the seeds of faith and hope, or of
bitterness and cynicism, are sown in childhood. I remember
one friend telling me that she had found it very difficult in
adult life to accept that there really was a life after death.
When she was quite a small girl her father, whom she had
loved intensely, died. From the moment of his death it was
as if an impenetrable wall had been erected, for his name
was never mentioned to her again by any of the family. She

felt in later life that this had been a deliberate attempt to help her forget her father so that the wound would heal. But it did not achieve this. The only thing it did was to induce her to form a belief that death must be the end of everything.

When bereavement comes a child's first need is not just a theory, or even an attempt at explanation of what death means. What he needs first of all is a sustaining affection, a sense of reassurance, a feeling of security. Strangely enough, it is often in supplying these needs that a widowed mother can help herself out of selfish grief. The very fact that her children need succour, need love, need *her* more than ever, helps her to find purpose again in life.

I think the bitterness can only be taken out of grief for children if they are helped to accept the truth that the real personality they loved still lives on, only now in the immediate presence of Christ.

One of our children, Maureen (aged ten when her Daddy died), was especially grieved at the thought of his body wasting and perishing away. His body was the part of him which had made him recognisable to her. She had loved his soft and gentle touch, his happy smile, his affectionate eyes. She could not bear to think these parts of him should just be destroyed.

I explained it to her in this way. I have a beautiful necklace, which, when it was first given to me, was in a very attractive box. The necklace is still beautiful but the box has long since worn out and has had to be discarded. A better box has been found to protect the necklace, but the thing of beauty, the really valuable thing, the necklace itself, is just as it ever was.

So it was with her Daddy. The person we all loved was more, far more, than the earthly body which clothed him for the years we had known him. What gave him his soft and gentle touch? What made his smile so happy? Why were his eyes so affectionate? Why, it was the personality, the thing of value, the real Daddy, who was housed within his earthly body—just as my necklace was housed within a temporary box.

Our earthly bodies sometimes become worn out with disease and pain, for our bodies are such that they suffer, and wear, and die. Yet the real person lives on, and if we have loved Christ we have a deeper and fuller life than we can ever imagine. I had found a better box to house my necklace. In God's good time their Daddy would be given a more perfect body by which we would recognise him in the life to come.

Maureen now tells me that there was another illustration I also used about a pet bird being freed from its cage. This illustration I probably borrowed from that gem of literature, Alexander Irvine's *My Lady of the Chimney Corner*. Anna, Alexander's mother, was trying to comfort Eliza Lecky on the sudden death of her son Henry. Liza kept on lamenting that Henry was gone, never to return. Anna, with her supreme wisdom and Irish quaintness, said to her, "Liza, it's just like this. When the spirit leaves the body, we say the body's dead, but it's just like a partnership gone broke. One goes up and the other down. To kiss a corpse is like kissing a cage when the bird inside has flown—there's nothing in it." (4)

Thus I was able to tell my children that at the moment when death finally came I was more sure than ever before that the word "Death" did not apply to those who have loved the Lord Jesus. I knew without doubt that though the loved personality was no longer within the earthly body, yet somewhere Walter was still very much alive. When the children and I talked together of him we were so sure that our relationship with him was not severed. It was altered, certainly. We could not communicate with him as we did when he was on earth, but we all had the sense of still being cared for, of being cherished.

I was sure that my children had grasped this great truth when I listened to one of them pray, on more than one occasion, many months after the bereavement, with great sincerity, "Thank you for giving us a Mummy and Daddy to love and care for us. Please bless all those poor children who have no Mummies and Daddies." It was so obvious that they did not regard themselves in the ordinary sense as having *no* Daddy, as children abandoned, unloved and unwanted do. For them he still exists. That does not mean that they do not miss his physical presence. There are moments of grief when the ground has to be covered all over again, but generally there seems to be an awareness that he is not permanently lost to them.

I think it is helpful to explain to children that the moment of death is not the harsh and terrible thing they often picture it to be. We cannot deny that the accidents and illnesses leading up to death are often terrifying and distressing, but the moment of passing itself is often as gentle as a sigh.

> *I heard the call, "Come follow,"*
> *   That was all.*
> *Earth's joys grew dim,*
> *My soul went after Him.*
> *I rose and followed.*
> *   That was all.*

I have encouraged my children to talk about their Daddy as much as they wish, and to recall the many happy incidents

53

of the past. They talk of happy occasions when we were all together; they remember a little rhyme he would be in the habit of reciting; a wild flower he had pointed out; a joke he had shared; an amusing habit he had had.

So it is by dwelling on the happy times we had together that the sad memories of his pain and suffering tend to fade. His influence is still in our home. He is not here to consult, but instinctively the children seem to know what he would have expected of them in a certain situation; what advice he would have given them on a particular problem; what joy he would have shown at a special achievement.

In the early days after our loss many a visitor to our home told me how they had come feeling embarrassment, wondering how they ought to act or speak before the children. Should they talk naturally, and express their sympathy for our grief? Or should they refrain from any mention of my husband when the children were around for fear of opening up a raw wound; for fear of tears and newly awakened sorrow? The visitors were seldom left long in doubt about what to do, for the children usually opened up the conversation themselves. They did not talk much about their Daddy's sufferings or death, but they would say, "Have you seen this photograph of Daddy? It is the one we like best. It was taken just before he took ill."

Or maybe it would be, "We are trying to keep this primula plant alive because it was one Daddy liked very much."

There were so many little things we did, as it were, for his sake. I never grew a plant in my life until after he died. But he loved plants, and he loved his garden and tended with great care all the things he had planted. So now we sow and plant and try to keep a tidy garden, and find great joy in doing it all in memory of him. Sometimes I feel if I were to see him again he would have a twinkle in his eyes, and he would say, "It looks as if I've bequeathed to you my green fingers."

To talk or write about one's grief is often to assuage it, especially where a child is concerned.

A good many months after Walter died our eldest child, Michael, showed me a composition he had written for his English master. It was entitled "My Hero". He had written simply and sincerely and movingly about his father's personality and attributes, climaxing his essay by a clear description of the heroism revealed in the last days of severe pain and deteriorating faculties.

Later on, when Maureen was asked to write on "The Most Memorable Day of my Life", quite spontaneously she wove her story round the joyous happenings of the morning when her Daddy had awakened with the words, "I am not going to die yet. God has still work for me to do."

Now I would like you to read what our youngest child, Rosalind, wrote in her school examinations, when she was eleven years old. The examination took place when she was remembering the fourth anniversary of her Daddy's death, and no doubt her thoughts had been for some days centred on the happenings of that fateful February.

A STRANGE DREAM

"It took me a long time to fall asleep that night. I had the 'flu, and was hot all over. But in time I fell into a deep sleep. Then all of a sudden I heard a voice. A small, tinkling whisper! 'Come and dance with me again, under the blossom of May, where the sun is bright and all pain is gone. Oh, won't you come and dance with me?'

"I, funnily enough, did not feel scared. I went with the invisible person, and he took me to somewhere wonderful. It was a lovely sort of city, with golden streets, and minstrels played.

I was awed with the most beautiful sight. Then a voice seemed to say, 'This is heaven.'

"I went back then to my home again. Mummy afterwards came into my room, and brought me my breakfast. She was having a hard job those days as my father was dangerously ill and I had the 'flu.

"That afternoon my father died, but I was not afraid, because I had a feeling that God had sent me that dream so that I would know that my father was being taken to a wonderful land, where God would take care of him, and he would not have to suffer those long days of pain. I am glad that I had that comforting dream, so that I would know Daddy would be well cared for.

"This is a true dream, and I think it is the strangest but best dream I have ever had. I know I will not be scared to die when the time comes."

*　　*　　*　　*

People say to me sometimes, "Do they never—do you never yourself—wonder why the period of recovery was so brief? Do any of you ever feel bitterness that disappointment and death followed so swiftly the period of promise?"

I think the answer we would all be inclined to give to that is that we feel so intensely grateful for those weeks of restoration that it would seem almost blasphemous to doubt God's wisdom in the final outcome. It is as if we all feel that God wanted the one we loved in the first instance, but He graciously gave him back to us for a brief while. That period, brief though it was, was gilded with the most celestial and eternal radiance, and we all feel, I think, that during it we were being fully equipped for the deep sorrow and dark night still ahead of us.

I remember the evening of Walter's death when our doctor came in to see us all. He said to me, "From our point of view you could have had Walter with you all these past months, but as a helpless and hopeless invalid. Instead, you had him with you as a useful person, able to do most of the tasks he wanted to do. That is something to be very thankful for."

That seemed to us to sum up the situation. God wanted Walter, and God in the end took him home. But not before He had added weeks of unexpected joy to our experience.

Of course we are all human, and for every day of sure and certain hope there are times of weakness and uncertainty when some of us go about stumbling blindly to find the light again. Whilst we remain subject to human frailty these things must be.

There are, as is only natural, periods of grief when I have to explain all over again that even if we are deprived of the presence of the one we love for twenty, or thirty, or forty years here on earth, yet that is really a very short while compared with eternity when we believe he will be available to us again. We sometimes feel that children, because of their immaturity, cannot possibly understand anything of the meaning of eternity. But "Heaven lies about us in our infancy", and I have come to see that a child's understanding of eternal matters is much deeper than we imagine.

Of course there were, and still are, many tricky questions to answer. In seeking to find answers, we must at the same time seek to satisfy a child's need for security and trust. There is no doubt that death can be for any child a terribly menacing thing, and unless the queries are handled gently, and with understanding, doubts and conflicts about the Love of God can cause acute agony. Everything must be interpreted in the light of God's love and care shown us in Christ Jesus.

"Why did God take our Daddy just when we needed him most?" There is no slick answer to such a question, for none of us can presume to know the mind of God. I told them

57

frankly I did not know. But I explained that my belief is that every unfinished service, every gift only partly used up, will find a new opportunity and renewal in the immediate presence of God. So perhaps it was that God required their Daddy for some special work in the life beyond the earthly one—work that we could not possibly comprehend or visualize.

Sometimes one of them would say, "Why did God take away our Daddy who was so good and kind to us, and leave other men who are cruel and unkind to their wives and families?"

Here again I had to explain that none of us really has the answer. But I told them that the Christian Church has always taught that sooner or later every person must meet God. Daddy was prepared and ready to meet Him, having sought forgiveness for all his imperfections, and having sought to live as he believed God would have desired. It would be harder for the men who were cruel and unkind to meet God's judgment. So was it not a good thing that these men still had some time left on earth to change their ways, and to seek God's forgiveness in order to be better prepared to meet Him?

The twenty-third Psalm is the Psalm of great comfort for adult and child alike. There is an American Indian version of this Shepherd's Psalm which I have found particularly attractive to children. When grief comes to us we never fail to find peace in the verses four, five and six. These are particularly beautiful and meaningful in the Red Indian rendering.

The Great Father above a Shepherd is, and with Him I want not.

He throws me out a rope, and the name of the rope is love, and He draws me to where the grass is green, and the water is not dangerous, and I eat and lie down satisfied.

Sometimes my heart is very weak and falls down, but He lifts me up again, and draws me into the good road. His name is Wonderful.

Sometime, it may be soon, it may be longer, it may be a long, long time, He will draw me into a place between the mountains. It is dark here, but I'll not draw back. I'll be afraid not, for it is there between the mountains, that the Shepherd Chief will meet me, and the hunger that I have felt all through this life will be satisfied. Sometimes He makes the love rope into a whip, but afterwards He gives me a staff to lean upon.

He spreads the table before me with all kinds of food. He puts His hand upon my head, and all the tired is gone. My cup He fills, until it is running over.

What I tell you is true. I lie not. These roads that are "away ahead" will stay with me through life. And afterwards I will go to live in the "Big Tepee", and sit down with the Shepherd Chief for ever.

6

New Horizons

IT WAS AN AFTERNOON of gaping loneliness just a few weeks after Walter's death. I felt crushed with grief. The Manse was empty, and I was gazing round at the study furniture, thinking wistfully of days gone by. I thought of the times when there had been the rich, wonderful, carefree sound of happy laughter in the room. The days, too, when we had much serious thought and discussion before a lecture or sermon. My mind went back also to the days so full of promise when I had occupied the study desk, scribbling away at the pages of *Queen of the Manse*.

I thought of the Epilogue to the book which I had written jauntily, with my tongue in my cheek, after an evening's fun.

"He opened his arms wide to me and said, 'Come here.'

"When I came he said, 'April 24th again. How many years have you been Queen of the Manse now?'

"'Fourteen,' I said.

"'And how do you like being a parson's wife?'

"'Well now,' I replied quizzically, 'since you happen to be the parson, I think I can manage to endure it for a wee while longer.'"

The irony of it all now! "I think I can manage to endure it for a wee while longer." Little had I realised when I penned those words just how very short would be the time left for me to be Queen of the Manse.

Now, around me lay books, sorted out for packing or disposal. Furniture was in disarray as I tried to decide what we could reasonably keep, and what would have to go. I was acutely aware that it would not be long before I was virtually homeless in a country where it is well-nigh impossible to find a suitable house to rent at a reasonable price. I was filled with dismay at the thought of the years ahead, when I would have to bear *singly* family responsibilities which were, in God's order, meant to be borne *jointly*.

Then, as I looked at the study desk again, there flashed into my mind the memory of an afternoon just before Christmas when I had been out shopping. Walter was listening to the radio, and when I returned home he told me how he had been greatly helped and strengthened by listening to a radio programme. It was *Silver Lining*, and the speaker had been a widow who had told of how she and her dying husband had found strength during weeks of sorrow and suffering.

After Walter told me about it he said, "Perhaps my story may be of help to someone, some day."

Now that conversation returned to me with a compelling urge to do something about it. As I gazed at the study desk I realised what could be the way out of my immediate grief. I was to use our experiences to try to help others walking the same troubled road.

I sat down at the typewriter. I am not a skilled typist, and always the task of typing is laborious. But that afternoon there was no great difficulty. I began the story of our experiences from the time when we had sung "Be still, my soul", and wrote on until the moment of death. The next day I sent the script off to Stuart Hibberd of the *Silver Lining* programme, exactly as I had composed it. A few weeks later I broadcast it without addition or subtraction. It was, as it stood, exactly the right length for the fifteen-minute programme.

This was my first B.B.C. talk, but since that day I have broadcast on a number of occasions. Normally, when I am preparing to write or speak, I like to spend many hours gathering the material, and many more on refining and polishing it. I am sure it would not be good for me to be able to produce a talk without this frequent revision, correction, deletion, shortening and lengthening. There is a discipline in this process which I enjoy and feel I need because it helps me to assess the value of what I have written.

But for my first *Silver Lining* talk, I feel there was a special inspiration. I was too emotionally exhausted after the strain of the previous weeks to contemplate long periods of revision and correction. I certainly could not have faced lengthy rehearsals or recordings at a B.B.C. studio. It seemed that God had enabled me, at the first attempt, to have correct in this talk the timing, phrasing, sequence and content as a token that my experiences could be, and would be, a help to others. It was just the incentive I needed, and that occasion opened the door to new friendships and opportunities which hitherto I should have thought impossible.

This book has grown out of some of these radio talks, because the resulting correspondence has revealed the number of sorrowing, perplexed, seeking people there are amongst the bereaved. There are many who find through writing to someone they have never met, a solace in emptying their hearts—catharsis is, I believe, the best word to describe this process of healing.

Often the greatest help which can be given to bereaved

persons is to allow them just to talk about their new situation again and again, until they can come to terms with their feelings. Sometimes near friends and relations are too closely involved in the bereavement to be of much help. A trusted minister can be of immense comfort, even by just listening, not once, but several times, to the story of despair, frustration and fear. Just by allowing bereaved souls to talk about their sorrow is to help them to come to the place where their emotions are manageable. And from that point they can learn to live more realistically, and to plan positively for their future.

A flexibility of help is required because each bereaved person is an individual, suffering individual agonies. There are widows who will change their minds too often about their future plans; there are those whose plans are perhaps too rigid and unreasonable where other members of the family are concerned; and there are some who, in their distress, seem quite incapable of making up their minds at all. All of these need help and tolerant understanding in making their adjustments, and courage to accept that all one's life after widowhood may seem to be spent in making re-adjustments.

There are so very many with questions to ask. Some, before writing to me, had asked elsewhere, sometimes of their minister, sometimes of people less qualified to give them an answer. Some had found the answer, but many were still groping for truth. Some, alas, in their search had turned to sub-Christian sects because they imagined they had found there a more definite and authoritative approach than their own church could offer, or had offered them. It was while pondering some of the questions asked in my correspondence that much of the remaining material for this book was gathered.

I am truly conscious in trying to answer people's questions that as a theologian I am very much an amateur, and I must here acknowledge my great debt to people like William Barclay, the authors of *Moffatt's New Testament Commentaries*, C. S. Lewis, F. W. Robertson and many others whose writings have helped me to formulate many of my beliefs. In some instances my views differ from these writers' interpretations, but so often they have been the ones who have set me off on a train of thought and helped me to understand the Bible more fully.

But most of all I feel that many of the conversations I had with Walter in the years of his active ministry, and many of the theological discussions we had both before and after his sermons, have helped me to compile much of the remaining material.

One of the first things which my early broadcast did for me was to cure any tendency to self-pity. I think that the most soul-destroying emotion which can come to a widow—indeed to any bereaved person—is self-pity. We have to learn how to deal with this crippling force, or there is a danger that the spirit will shrivel, and cynicism, bitterness and rebellion will result.

Self-pity disappears when we realise that we are not unique in our bereavement. This thought came forcibly to me just after my first broadcast when I read one of the resulting letters. It was from a clergyman, still young, with small children of his own. He has given me permission to tell his story. He was compelled to spend the rest of his life in a wheel-chair because of a progressive, crippling disease. In the *Silver Lining* broadcast following mine he had planned to speak with his wife about how they had been sustained in trials and illnesses. But as he listened to my talk his wife was dying of the same dread disease which had stricken Walter. Before his talk went on the air she had died, and he was left the occupant of a wheel-chair to care for two young children.

As I pen these words I have just been listening to him again. He spoke of God's sustaining power during the dark days following his wife's death. God did not leave him and his young children comfortless, for they have all found new happiness in the provision of a new partner and mother.

Yes, self-pity disappears when we realise that we are not unique in our bereavement. I found I was soon able to count the blessings still left to me. I had health and strength. I had three affectionate children to make life still worthwhile. I had a wealth of happy memories for lonely hours ahead. I had a profession to which I could eventually return. And I had the thrilling hope of reunion.

There are times, of course, when grief overwhelms us, and it is helpful then to make use of various practical aids to help lift us out of the dark pit of depression. The surest way out of grief is to try to use the experience gained to help someone else. But until we are in a fit frame of mind to do this it is possible to bury oneself in work so that time passes quickly, and physical tiredness brings much-desired sleep.

It is possible, too, to seek the company of sympathetic friends. But here we must be careful not to bore them eternally with our woes and complaints, or their sympathy will soon wear thin. We should, even in the early days after a bereavement, feel that we still belong to society; that we are still part of the world going relentlessly on around us. There is in the early days of sorrow a tendency to want to withdraw from company, yet I am sure that this is the time when one's home and one's heart should be opened wide to friends. There is a deepening of love and a forging of ties at this time just because suffering encourages in all of us a new tenderness and warmth of affection.

65

Some people feel, mistakenly I am sure, that in the early months after bereavement it is wrong to indulge in even the simplest pleasures. With the numbness and pain of death, this is in a way natural. But, especially where there are children, it is better to accept what simple joys are still available. This must sometimes be done even at the cost of disapproval from others, perhaps old friends.

I remember some weeks after Walter's death, when we were in the throes of trying to settle into a new home, there dawned one glorious day of blazing sunshine. I suggested that we should leave all the work and go to the seaside for a bathe and a picnic. We were enjoying the sunshine and the sea when an acquaintance, whom we had not seen since our bereavement, passed and spoke to us. I could tell from his demeanour and discomfiture that he was rather shocked to see us all picnicking in a rather carefree manner. I could almost hear him say, "It has not taken her long to get over it." A few weeks later a mutual friend said to me, "G . . . told me of seeing you all on the beach. But there, I suppose you felt that Walter would have approved."

Again there was the veiled disapproval which I could scarcely comprehend. Later, I came to think that we were living mentally and spiritually in separate generations, and that this attitude dated back to the time when long periods of mourning, with all-black attire, were observed. At the moment, however, I was too dumbfounded to comment, but inwardly I said to myself, "Walter most certainly would have approved—and heartily!" I could not for the life of me see anything Christian about sitting indoors moping on the first really hot and glorious day of spring. But it is difficult to explain that sort of thing, anyway, to narrow and censorious people. We do sorrow—but not as others who are without hope.

Fortunately there are numerous friends just longing to be helpful after a bereavement—yearning to do some little thing which will be of practical assistance. All too often we shrink from accepting that help. We want to be independent. We are scared of losing face or dignity. I have had to pray many times that God would give me the grace to receive help with the same courtesy as I would offer it. It is so much easier to be gracious when giving in such circumstances than it is when receiving. We must learn, through acceptance of generosity, as well as through practising generosity, to become part of the great fellowship of suffering.

So it is that work and companionship bring relief, but not, I find, lasting relief. There is only one thing that can do that, and that is an indestructible relationship with Jesus Christ. He is the only one truly equipped to heal the brokenhearted, and to bind up the wounded spirit. In the days of our prosperity we believed the promise in Philippians 4— the one Walter had preached about. In the days of our adversity we both had proved that by taking every trouble and care to the Lord in prayer, peace, which was greater than our human understanding, came again in an inexplicable way.

I love to entertain, and to be entertained. I enjoy immensely being in the company of friends. I enjoy work. But best of all I love to be alone with God, and I find that through fellowship with Him, through His word, and through prayer, I can reach the only sure path to true healing and solace.

7

Remorse

IF SELF-PITY is a soul-destroying emotion, remorse is no less so. There is not a more deadly canker which can eat into the heart of a bereaved person. Even where a home has been supremely happy, in moments of sadness and depression following a death there tend to come flooding in thoughts of kindnesses left undone; memories of hasty words spoken, and then regretted; careless, hurtful, little actions. In periods of aloneness it is all too easy to brood over these defects, and it is all too possible to become unhealthily introspective.

I have recently been reading an autobiography by an eminent Christian. He looks back on a long married life, and says he is grateful to God that he has no regrets, and no unhappy memories of strifes and tensions in his home life. This is no doubt very beautiful for him, but I could not help but feel as I read his words that they were particularly unhelpful to anyone struggling with the agonies of remorse. His bliss would only serve to accentuate one's own regrets, and memories of strifes and tensions of the past. God alone knows how many are trying to fight a lone battle with remorse. I have been made aware, through some of my *Silver Lining* correspondence, just how terrifying the struggle can be for some people.

When I wrote *Queen of the Manse* I told of my belief that

if two people are to live every day, and every part of every day, in complete and absolute harmony it would be necessary for them either to be sub-normal or over-civilised. I suppose there are some such couples, but I have never met them. I am not so sure that they would be all that interesting to meet either.

Marriage is not unadulterated happiness. In every union there are many disaffections, as well as affinities. The unhappy marriage is where the couple have allowed their animosities to outweigh their affinities; where they have refused to learn to tackle their problems together. The happy marriage is where the things on which a couple unite outweigh the disunities.

Even in the very happiest of unions it must be extremely rare for any partner to be able to look back with absolutely no moments of regret.

How does one deal with remorse? There are three main stages, I think, in coping with it. And one thing is certain. It must be dealt with at once or life will become bitter.

The first thing to remember is that were the loved one back again he would hold no grudge against us for our imperfections or human frailty. He would want us to forget all our niggling regrets as he will already have done.

I have found that it helps to try to picture, for a moment, what it would be like to meet my husband again face to face. I would say, "Do you remember that occasion? Well, I'm sorry about it." I can then easily picture a familiar gesture of his when he would place his hand on my shoulder and say, "Why, I'd forgotten all about that. Now you just forget about it too, and think of all our happy moments together."

Following this, of course, we must take all our misdeeds and imperfections to God in prayer, and accept His mercy and forgiveness. God knows only too well that some of the things we have done are no light misdemeanours to be glossed over and repressed. But we cannot put the clock back and relive the past, however much we would wish it. There is a tremendous burden lifted when we realise that it is futile to spend time and thought and energy dwelling on things we cannot alter now. Where sin abounds, grace does much more abound. Christ's forgiveness is freely ours if we will accept it. Indeed, we must come humbly to the place where we realise that there is nothing left for us to do but accept His forgiveness.

Apart from Judas, Peter must have suffered remorse more than any other person associated with Christ. Peter discovered the cure for remorse was not self-lashing. It was to go forward beyond guilt to the place of self-knowledge, humility and forgiveness. We must all learn how to heal our self-despisings; how to pluck from the heart that rooted sorrow.

Judas dealt with his remorse in a wrong and bitter way. He destroyed himself. But I cannot believe that by doing so he also destroyed his remorse. It would, I feel sure, be still a part of him in his state after death.

Peter's sorrow, after denying his Lord so near, so very near to the time of the Crucifixion, must have been agony beyond words. Could he ever forget the look the Lord gave him when he uttered the words of denial? I think not. But he used the way of peace available to each one of us—the way of forgiveness. What years of usefulness would have been wasted in the service of his Master if he had spent the days following our Lord's Passion lashing himself unmercifully for his crass cowardice and disloyalty.

After seeking Christ's forgiveness Peter must have embarked on the third stage of dealing with remorse—a very important stage which so many bereaved people forget.

Having accepted forgiveness from those we love, and from God, it is very necessary to forgive ourselves.

When these stages have been gone through, we discover that the heart begins to be made whole again. A fourth stage then readily follows. We can never really atone for mistakes of the past by good deeds in the future. But once we have learnt the bitterness of remorse there is an added incentive to treat with true charity and loving kindness those who are still left in our care.

When self-pity and remorse are allowed to rule, the bereaved person is all too often heard to say that life now has lost all meaning and purpose. We need not find it so. Indeed there are things which should hold deeper meaning for us after bereavement. This is especially so where the festivals of the Church year are concerned.

At Christmas one tends at first to be wistful, and to think only of the vacant chair. But with the thought of the real meaning of Christmas it becomes not just a season of regrets and longings, but of intense joy.

Light and Life to all He brings,
Risen with healing in His wings.
Mild He lays His glory by;
Born that man no more may die.

"Born that man no more may die." Christ came that first Christmas so that the terror of death might be removed. Since then, for those who belong to the Christ of God, there is no death.

Then comes Easter, with all its glad hope and renewed life, and its promise of personal immortality. The joy of the Resurrection becomes a real and vital thing. Because He lives we shall live also.

After Easter there is Whitsuntide. When Jesus went away from His disciples they were sad and questioning and bewildered. But Christ promised that they would not be alone. The Holy Spirit would come to them as their Comforter and Strengthener. Neither are we left alone in our bereavement. He is our Comforter and Strengthener also.

8

Where are they now?

WHERE ARE THEY NOW? I suppose this is the question, uttered or unexpressed, of every person who has witnessed the passing of someone he has loved dearly.

We must not push our enquiries into unseen things beyond what God permits us to know. But it is nevertheless possible to combine a reverent curiosity with a healthy reserve. For though Eternity is largely a mystery to us, it is not wholly beyond comprehension. There are some things revealed in Scripture which help us to picture something of the life hereafter. It is well to remember, though, that we are limited in our thinking because we can only comprehend Eternity in terms of time and space, and the senses which are available to us here on earth. It is quite possible, indeed I think it is very probable, that there are other senses which we know nothing of, but which will be in full use in the life to come.

In this scientific age the trouble is we are always seeking definite proofs, and of course life after death can never be proved scientifically. Science has done a great deal for us. It has helped in many cases to heal a broken body. But it cannot heal a broken heart. We are more than body, and we are more than mere intellect and will. As long as we have our hopes and fears, our joys and our sorrows, so long shall we need assurance and consolation — things which science

73

cannot offer. The Christian attitude to death and grief is, I feel sure, the only one which can give inward support and spiritual strength. In almost every matter relating to the spirit we have to accept much on faith. All profound religion is mystical, but when we take that leap of faith we find that there are aids in abundance which confirm and assure us. God's Word, as found in the Bible, is one of these sure strengtheners of our faith.

I shall keep for ever the memory of that first moment after Walter's death. I was whispering to myself, "If only I could be sure of what is happening to him now." Immediately there flashed into my mind almost as if spoken by a voice, the words, "And the angels carried him to Abraham's bosom."

Later on I looked up these words, which are found in Luke's Gospel, 16:22. They were spoken by our Lord during one of His parables, the one usually called The Rich Man (or Dives) and Lazarus. Christ is describing what happened to the poor man Lazaraus after he died. As the words flashed into my mind at Walter's death, my heart was filled with a sense of assurance, because, though my human mind could not grasp it all, I was convinced that someone was ministering to his needs. I felt sure that he was entering Christ's presence

This experience was a very illuminating and strengthening one for me. But sometimes when I have mentioned it to people who are sceptical about a vivid, conscious life here-after, they have thought it wise to warn me that it is not always safe to take parabolic sayings and try to build doctrine or truth upon them. However, even allowing these words as a piece of poetic imagery, they are still our Lord's words, and contain certain truth. Incidentally, it is interesting to note that this is the only instance where a character in one of our Lord's parables is given a name—a name which means "God is my help".[1]

The words "And the angels carried him into Abraham's bosom" seem to convey quite clearly that the soul leaving this world, with its trust in God, does not go out solitary into a great and lone land. I knew that afternoon of Walter's death that, though he had passed beyond the point where I could minister to him, there were others—perhaps angels —who were ministering to his immediate needs.

I believe if we could grasp this it would remove from us a great deal of the fear of death. Psychiatrists say that this is the greatest fear common to man. The fear is, I think, a combined one—the dread of loneliness, the terror of the unknown, and the burden which comes with a sense of sin. Victory over this fear comes when we realise that Death and Sin were both conquered in Christ's own death and resurrection.

When we plan to visit an unknown country we are often filled with doubts because of the many unforeseen hazards and pitfalls. But perhaps, more than that, we are filled with the fear of a terrible loneliness, away from kith and kin. How different it is if we know there is someone in that unknown country awaiting our arrival; someone who will be there to guide and direct. God saves man from the terror of isolation which is the extreme loneliness of death. Not only are there, seemingly, angels to minister to our needs, but the loved ones gone before are there too. Best of all, Christ is there.

I was once in the company of a glib young man, self-assured, polished, witty, original, but blatantly ignorant regarding many great matters. Amongst many revealing statements which he dropped that evening (when speaking of

[1] Wm. Barclay's commentary.

75

subjects which were to me eternal truths) he said this: "I don't know where I came from. I don't know where I'm going. What's more, I don't care." My inward thoughts, as I listened, were these. "Young man, you are merely stating that you have never cared for anyone very deeply. Or, if you have, you have never lost the one you cared for." When we have loved and lost, then our experience is necessarily that much deeper and fuller and richer. For however little we might care about our own future, yet if we have loved deeply, we shall care deeply about what has happened, or is happening to those who have left us.

In very few societies is death simply regarded as an exit from the world with no continuance of personality. Even in primitive cultures the part of personality referred to as soul or spirit is held to persist hereafter. But the bereaved person does not want merely a bare, logical, universal argument that the one he has loved survives death. We are not interested merely in immortality, merely in survival; nor should we wish the life to come to be just an extension of human experience here. The whole teaching about the life hereafter takes on new beauty when we think of it in Paul's words: "Absent from the body; present with the Lord" (2 Cor. 5: 8). I want to write more of this exhilarating truth later.

Someone has said that the great difference between death and all other forms of human experience lies in this—that we are given no information about it. "The dead man is wise, but he is silent. We cannot wring his secret from him."

There are only three recorded instances where Christ restored dead people to life again, and we do not learn much from these three personalities about the secrets of life beyond this earth. Mark preserves for us in his Gospel, chapter 5, the story of the raising of Jairus's daughter (see also Luke 8 and Matthew 9). In Luke 7 we read about the raising of the widow's son at Nain, and in John 11 we have the thrilling story of the resurrection of Lazarus.

It is interesting to note that in two of these stories—that of Jairus's daughter, and Lazarus—Jesus seemed at first to resist the appeal of affection, and He did not rush to the scene of the sorrow and bereavement. But when He did appear, it was in the fulness of that exalted power over life and death, which is the characteristic of the Lord God Himself. This is the Christ who has ever since been the centre of the Church's faith and love.

None of the three main characters in these miracle stories gives us any indication of what life was like on the other side. This to me is not altogether surprising. As I have already indicated, I believe that in the hereafter we shall have senses and faculties of which we know nothing here. Time and space will not have the same meaning for us. We shall, I think, have faculties for acquiring knowledge of which we now have no conception. It is perhaps understandable that these three returning from a life beyond would not be able, when humanly restricted, even to remember what had transpired, or to put it in human language if they could remember.

H. G. Wells tells a story based on a legend about a lost valley in Switzerland where some disease raged which made every child blind from birth. One man who could see eventually found his way into the valley, and tried to converse with the inhabitants. But words like "look", "see", "eyes", "sight", meant nothing to them, and they thought he was mentally unbalanced. After studying him for some weeks, they decided that his brain must somehow be affected by these strange things called "Eyes" and they felt that the only way to make him "normal" again, that is, like themselves, was to gouge out his eyes and make him blind.

We are, in a spiritual sense, like the inhabitants of that

legendary Swiss valley. If someone were to return and try to explain to us the wonders of that land beyond, he would find he was without human vocabulary to describe it. Our human limitations would prevent our full understanding of the beauty of it all.

In recent times I have been interested to read the experiences of some, who, by heart massage or other medical means, have been "brought back from the dead". Several of them seem to have had similar experiences. One patient called Rose told her husband something which seemed to be rather typical of all the others. She said that she had had a wonderful dream of great beauty, but the details of this dream she could never remember afterwards.

Mrs. Ann Armstrong, who calls herself a "responaut", as she depends on an iron lung for life, wrote a moving article in *The Guardian* on December 30th, 1963.

"The time was Advent, 1955. The poliomyelitis virus was obviously enjoying his stay with me. The doctors and nurses stood helplessly by as the paralysis crept farther and farther over my body. . . .

"When I 'died' I found myself in a place that was all joy and delight. Everywhere was green and I was not aware of my body at all. I knew I was seeking a gate, and as I moved happily through this green place I knew that the gate was small and made of wood. I had almost reached it, and I knew that once I had passed through it I should know this joy and peace for ever.

"Then I heard my children's names and I stopped, and at the point of listening I heard their names again, and in that moment of time, when I was being born again into eternity, I turned back. . . .

"The sick imaginings of a paralysed woman perhaps, you will say. I remember much of my delirium, but this experience was different. It happened after the fever had passed. . . .

78

"Now for me, time, like gravity, is a force which holds me to this planet—death is the cervix through which I must be born to find my way again to that far country from which I have returned.

"This, then, is my story. There was no golden gate, no new Jerusalem, only the little wooden gate of the Cross." (5)

I think it is of value to note that in each case where Jesus raised a person from the dead, it was out of great compassion for the person bereft, rather than for the one who had died. If the life hereafter is as wonderful as we believe it will be, then not one of us would wish back again, for their own sakes, those of our loved ones who have died in Christ. When Lazarus was raised, Christ showed deep affection and pity for both Mary and Martha. Sympathy for the lonely widow who had lost her only son, was obvious in the raising at Nain. A father's grief for a loved child was what seemed to influence our Lord at the raising of Jairus's daughter. But it is essential to remember that towering over even this deep and compassionate understanding of a sorrowing heart was Christ's supreme desire to glorify God, and to enable others to believe and to see the glory of God.

But we can receive great comfort from the fact that Jesus Christ has a part in our sorrows. There is great pathos in the words of the story about the widow of Nain's son. "He was his mother's only son, and she was a widow." The word "compassion" used to describe Christ indicates He was moved to the depths of His heart, and this is not the only occasion that this was so. In Matthew 14: 14 the same word is used when Jesus looked upon the many sick. In Matthew 15: 32 the thought of people suffering hunger again moved Him to the depths of His being. In Mark 1: 41 the same word is used to describe His feelings towards a leper. We could go on enumerating similar instances. We can truly receive great comfort from the fact that Jesus has a part in our sorrows.

Yet our greatest hope is not in Christ's compassion but in Christ's power. As we read these stories we are filled with a burning wistfulness that Christ should do the same for us. But what we desperately need is a recognition that death *is* subservient to the power of Christ. He is the Lord of life, and of death.

Clearly, if we are to learn anything about the state of our loved ones in the near hereafter, we must look beyond the experiences of the three characters in the Bible miracles. Yet there is one important point we should note. The personal identity of all three persons raised had been preserved through the ordeal of death.

If we return to our Lord's parable about Dives and Lazarus, there are some things we can deduce, even if the story is regarded as an incomplete revelation of life after death. First of all, our Lord assumes a conscious life hereafter in which the two men's existence goes on uninterrupted. The life after death seems to be the natural continuation of the earthly life. I do not want here to deal with the division of the ways which were taken by Lazarus and Dives. This is a difficult and painful subject which I must touch on later because it cannot, and should not be ignored.

"Abraham's bosom" mentioned in the parable is simply a Jewish phrase for the place of rest and joy prepared for those who have lived and died in the faith.

Some things we may deduce from the story. Both Lazarus and Dives are represented as being alive, capable of thinking, speaking, feeling, remembering. Their life is still one of awareness.

In the moments immediately following a death, we all, I think, ask much the same questions. "Does he still remember? Does he still care?" Here we need not be bound by sentimental guessing. Without indulging in foolish misrepresentation of the future state, it is clear that Scripture is much more definite than we often tend to be. Dives and Lazarus both remembered, and they both cared.

Of even greater value to the seeker is the story of the Transfiguration in Luke 9, Mark 9 and Matthew 17. Here the veil of material reality is rent, and the disciples are permitted for a brief while to see into the spiritual world. Moses and Elijah return for a brief period from the Unseen Life, and speak on the Mount with Christ. They must have been conscious and interested spectators of the happenings on earth, and they certainly knew of the plan for the redemption of the world.

Moses and Elijah were two of the most prominent of Old Testament characters. They are mentioned later in Hebrews as being amongst those who have died in the faith. Moses had been the Law-giver, and Elijah had been the prophet. According to Old Testament stories, Moses had not reached the Promised Land during his earthly life, so unless there were other meetings with Christ on the Mount, which were not witnessed, this would have been Moses's first visit to the Holy Land. Elijah, on the other hand, knew the country well.

Moses had died a sad man, with promises unfulfilled, and his life's work uncompleted. Elijah had been translated after his experience under the juniper tree at a time when his people were living in idolatry. Their life's work had been unfinished, but now they had the promise of accomplishment in Christ Himself.

Some things we can infer from the meeting of Moses and Elijah with Jesus. First of all they are described as being two *men* (Luke's account). In other words, they were basically the same type of being as they were on earth. Not only that, but they were men able to converse, able to understand clearly the redemptive process. Indeed, they understood it more clearly than any who lived on earth. They were enjoying what would appear to be a continuity of existence with enlarged powers.

We are not told how Peter, James and John recognised Moses and Elijah, but the fact that they were able to identify them would infer that personal identity is preserved in the world beyond. If the three disciples recognised these two, whom they had never met in the flesh, is it not reasonable to assume that we shall recognise our own loved ones when we meet them again?

Some people, who have corresponded with me after broadcast talks, have asked how we can reconcile this belief in a conscious life of knowledge hereafter with the fact that, even in the Bible, the word "sleep" is often used to describe death. It is quite true that in several passages death is spoken of as sleep: e.g. Matthew 9: 24; Acts 7: 60; 1 Thessalonians 4: 13; and 1 Corinthians 15: 6.

In the story of the raising of Jairus's daughter, Christ Himself says, "The child is not dead, but asleep." Clearly He is not speaking of a natural sleep. At least the evangelist does not take it as a literal sleep, or else there just would not have been any miracle to report. Before raising Lazarus Christ again mentions the word sleep. What, therefore, is meant? Is there any contradiction?

I do not think so. It seems to me that when the word sleep is used of death it is solely with reference to the body. Even in a natural earthly sleep there are parts of the mind which work on. Sleep is rarely a blank unconsciousness. The soul of man, severed from the body in death, lives on, and when we speak of those we love being "asleep in Christ", I take it as a parable. Earthly sleep, though it may mean great mental activity, largely precludes intercourse with the outside world.

So in the sleep of death there is necessarily a severance of communication with those on earth.

Of course, there are points at which all analogies break down. When we speak of our loved ones being "asleep", I do not think we need to adopt the crudely materialistic view that the actual earthly bodies they have possessed will be wakened up in resurrection. God has something better in store for us than that, and I would like to deal more fully with this in a later chapter.

There are two other passages which indicate, beyond doubt, that what we call death is not really a cessation of life. One is from Mark 12 (also Matthew 22, and Luke 20) where Christ says to the Sadducees, "I am the God of Abraham, Isaac and Jacob. God is not a God of the dead, but of the living." A certain declaration that Abraham, Isaac and Jacob are living still.

Christ also says words of great importance to Martha after her brother Lazarus had died. "I am the Resurrection and the Life. He that believeth on Me, though he die, yet shall he live." He did not say, "Yet shall he live *again*" in the sense of being raised up at the Last Day. He said, "Yet shall he live." This is the Messiah speaking, the Son of God, the One Whose coming ensures, for those who trust Him, that death has no sting, and the grave no victory. Here is something greater than sympathy. Here is light to illumine our darkness. The God Whom Christ revealed is such—Creator, Lord and God—that such a physical event as death cannot interrupt communion between Himself and His children. They are His, and His always, and they shall never die.

9

Till He Come

THE QUESTION often asked by bereaved folk who crave to know something about those they have lost—even if they regard the loss as merely temporary—is this: "Are they in their final and permanent state?" This is a question that has often been shelved by teachers in the Protestant churches because of the fear of being involved in Roman Catholic doctrine of purgatory. Throughout the ages there certainly have been abuses of the Church's doctrine of the Intermediate Life, but we must be careful, in sweeping away the falsehood, not to get rid also of the underlying truth.

The Christian Church is not of one mind concerning the present position of the departed. Some Christians believe that the words of Jesus, "Today shalt thou be with me in paradise" (Luke 23: 43), mean that the faithful immediately enjoy the bliss of being in His presence; the parable of Dives and Lazarus (Luke 16) might be taken as a support for this view.

Other Christians believe in a state of Purgatory, as a period of cleansing, or preparation for life in the presence of the Risen Christ. Yet others believe that the departed are disembodied spirits waiting in a state of unconsciousness for the Last Day, the Day of the Lord, or the Second Advent.

This Last Day is the time regarded as the end of history when the ultimate consummation will affect, not only the individual, but also society as a whole. It will mean the restoration of entire creation to a harmonious, unified life in Christ. Of the resurrection body given to those who are Christ's I want to write more in a later chapter. Meanwhile what is happening to those who have died? Perhaps we can learn something from the information available to us regarding the interval between Christ's Crucifixion and His Resurrection. Right from the earliest days of the Christian era, questions must have been posed regarding the days between.

The first hint of an answer is to be found in Paul's Epistle to the Ephesians, chapter 4 : 9, 10.

"Now that He ascended, what is it but that He also descended first into the lower parts of the earth? He that descended is the same also that ascended up, far above all heavens, that He might fill all things."

It is estimated that the Epistle of Peter was written some thirty years after this Ephesian Epistle, and in 1 Peter we have a firm statement which was eventually incorporated into the Apostle's Creed in the words, "He descended into Hell (Hades)."

The words from Peter read :

"For Christ also hath once suffered for sins, the just for the unjust, that He might bring us to God, being put to death in the flesh, but quickened by the Spirit : by which also He went and preached unto the spirits in prison; which sometime were disobedient, when once the long-suffering of God waited in the days of Noah, while the ark was preparing, wherein few, that is, eight souls were saved by water" (1 Peter 3 : 18–20).

85

"For for this cause was the gospel preached also to them that are dead, that they might be judged according to men in the flesh, but live according to God in the Spirit" (1 Peter 4: 6).

It is interesting to note that only one person could have revealed to the Apostles what happened to Christ in the intervening days between His death and resurrection. Christ must have made the revelation Himself.

Christ had come for man's salvation. But what of those who had lived before His coming? The early Christian belief seems to be that by Christ's entry into Hades the gospel was carried to them, and so He revealed Himself as Lord, not only of heaven and earth, but of Hades as well.

The Jews and Greeks held somewhat similar conceptions of the unseen world, the common abode of departed souls. The Jews called it Sheol, and the Greeks called it Hades. Sheol is the Old Testament word, and Hades is the New Testament word. Both words have at times been translated as our English word Hell which often creates a wrong conception unless the meanings and background of the word are studied.

One of the prophecies in the Old Testament is translated in Psalm 16: 10, as, "For Thou wilt not leave my soul in hell (Sheol)." This prophecy is again referred to in Acts 2: 27 in the same words.

Hades, or Sheol, was a dark and mysterious place until Christ lifted the veil a little. The Rabbis taught that Sheol was the common abode of all departed souls, just and unjust alike. But it was always thought of as being divided into two parts. The teaching was that the abodes of the blessed and the doomed were near to one another, but Christ, who used the word Hades in the parable of Dives and Lazarus where He also spoke of "Abraham's bosom", indicates that there is a great gulf between the two (Luke 16: 23, 26).

The two abodes were called Paradise and Gehenna. The word Paradise is used by Christ Himself at the time of His Crucifixion (Luke 23: 43). The dying thief had asked Christ to remember him when He came into His kingdom. Christ's reply was, "Today shalt thou be with me in paradise." In Christ's own hour of extreme loneliness, He was declaring in fact, that after death, and immediately afterwards, this repentant thief would be with Him in the realm of departed spirits, and in that part reserved for those who have been made just. We can, in asking what happened to the repentant thief after death, reply emphatically—Christ met him there. He was with the King in Paradise.

Paradise is a Persian word meaning "park" or "garden". This is the only occasion where Christ uses the expression, and there is certainly no support here, or elsewhere in the New Testament, for speculation about Paradise being a sort of Purgatory.

The part of Sheol regarded as being reserved for the wicked was called Gehenna, or Ge-Hinnom, or the Valley of Hinnom. The Valley of Hinnom lay to the south-west of Jerusalem, and in the reign of Ahaz had been polluted by fire-worship and human sacrifice (2 Kings 16: 3, 4; 2 Chronicles 28: 3). In consequence of this, it was set apart as the place where the refuse from the city should be burnt. In time the name came to be applied to the place of future punishment (*see* Jeremiah 7: 31–33, and Isaiah 66: 24). In the New Testament it is also referred to in Mark 9: 43–48.

The insights of the Old Testament are deepened in the New Testament, and the death and resurrection of Christ transform all our thinking about death. Before His own death Christ, in the parable of Dives and Lazarus, speaks of Lazarus being "comforted" after the difficult trials on earth. The greatest hope and light, however, come for us after

Christ's own "exodus", as His death was referred to. Stephen prays in Acts 7: 59, "Lord Jesus, receive my spirit." Paul speaks in Philippians 1: 23, as departing to be with Christ, which is far better. And in verse 21 of the same chapter he says, "For to me to live is Christ, to die is gain."

"Absent from the body, present with the Lord" are the words used in 2 Corinthians 5: 8.

"Blessed are the dead which die in the Lord" are the words in Revelation 14: 13.

Somehow the presence of Christ is vouchsafed to us in that waiting land. Our relationship with Christ is one which is independent of time, of place, of circumstances, even of death. Death cannot bring the believer into any situation, or any abode, which means separation from God.

So the Christian view of the life after death is not a picture of an unreal existence in hades, but a continuation of fellowship with Christ in His nearer presence, awaiting the Last Day. There is little in the way of precise and detailed information regarding the explicit character of this existence in Christ's presence. We can only rest assured that it is far better than our present state.

The future loses some of its dim and inscrutable mystery when we listen to our Lord's words to His disciples before His death. They are amongst the best-loved words in the whole of Scripture, and are to be found in John 14:

> "Let not your heart be troubled; ye believe in God, believe also in Me. In My Father's house are many mansions; if it were not so, I would have told you. I go to prepare a place for you."

We do not know a great deal about that place. But we do know—and this should be sufficient—that *He* is making it ready for us.

10

Communion of Saints

A FEW DAYS after Walter died a friend said to me, "If they are with Christ, and Christ is with us, then they cannot be very far away." A little later I read the same thought in a verse which conveys something of the nearness of our departed:

> *Death hides, but it does not divide.*
> *Thou art but on Christ's other side;*
> *Thou art with Christ, and Christ with me.*
> *In Him I still am close to thee.*

The hope of reunion one future day is sometimes but poor consolation for the bereft heart. Heavy theological arguments are also poor solace when our greatest craving is for the touch of a vanished hand, and for the sound of a voice that is still.

I know only too well how strong can be the longing for some sort of contact with those we love. I know the overwhelming desire to be able to ask advice, to tap the wisdom of those we have once partnered. Sometimes, when I have a major decision to make, I think of the clear and imaginative mind which was Walter's; the assurance he always displayed without any show of arrogance; the dignity and poise; the composure and the intellectual humility. I think often of his integrity and charity; his tolerance, his charm, his generosity, his courage and his leadership. And in thinking of these qualities, and so many more, I often voice the thought inwardly, "If only he were here now."

One day I was thinking along these lines when I took out from a bookcase a volume which I had given to Walter on his birthday, some ten years after our marriage. As I turned to the fly-leaf, I read words I had written there:

> For me, 'twas not the truth you taught,
> To you so clear, to me so dim;
> But when you came to me,
> You brought a sense of Him.
>
> And from your eyes He beckons me,
> And from your lips, His love is shed,
> Till I lose sight of you,
> And see the Christ instead.[1]

As I read those words again I felt immeasurably rebuked at my desire for communication. I remembered how often Walter had said to me that the real value of any word preached, any act of worship, any action, any life lived, was that it should direct men's attention away from the human being involved in the preaching, the action, the life, and focus their attention instead on God, and on His majesty and power.

Often the desire to communicate with those we love is born out of the fact that we are really putting that person before God. Attempts at communication stem from a sub-Christian approach to our problem. We have, perhaps, some major

---

[1] As my book goes to press, I am unable to trace the writer of these words. If the source is discovered I will make due acknowledgment in the next edition.

issue to decide, and we long for the opinion of a loved partner. We stand at a cross-road in life, and we know how once the decision would have been much easier when the wisdom of another, allied with our own judgment, would have helped us to make up our minds.

But, whatever the wisdom of that loved one, still it was a human wisdom, and always inferior to the wisdom and guidance of God. We can go in simple faith to God, through Christ, knowing that He will supply all the wisdom we require. If we come to any task or decision straight from the presence of God, we are not coming to it alone. No undertaking will then be too great for us. Our failure to cope, and our fears of not being able to cope, are in the main due to the fact that we try to do things *without* the assistance of God.

Man's greatest temptation is to guide himself by what he can see, feel and handle. That is why we so often try to see our loved ones in tangible form. If we do try that we are engaging in a practice that is less than Christian, for whatever the Communion of Saints is, it is not communication. There is a vast difference between trying to communicate with the dead, and communing with them.

The thought right throughout Scripture is that the dead may not return to earth, but the living must eventually go to them (2 Samuel 12 : 23). The art of "calling up the dead" was regarded as being contrary to God's will (1 Samuel 28). Communication was very sternly denounced in passages such as Isaiah 8 : 19 and Deuteronomy 18 : 9–11. Indeed, the inference throughout was that communication was attempted when men were away from God.

Attempts at communication can lead to a greater sense of frustration and forlorn desolation than the bereaved person feels already. I am convinced that with such attempts there is grave risk, and indeed peril.

But, having said that, I must say also that it seems to me that the Christian Church could, and ought to give some more definite teaching on what the Communion of Saints really means. As I have already mentioned, throughout the years since the Reformation many sections of the Church have neglected to explain what the doctrine means, because in pre-Reformation days there was the corruption of the teaching which led to many heresies.

Since Walter's death I have made enquiries of ministers in various sections of the Church, and I have come to the reluctant conclusion that many, though they hold the doctrine, hold it in a hesitating and ineffectual way. Whilst much is hidden from us, we must not be vague and shadowy and timid about what information is available to us.

Admittedly, it is a difficult doctrine to explain. And even when we come, through experience, to have a grasp of what it really means, we are obliged to say, with the Scots, that it is something "better felt than telt".

One of my children brought home to me rather forcibly something of the difference between communication and communion. She was reading an annual in which were instructions for making a work box. The first words were, "Ask your father to cut you a piece of wood with measurements . . ." My daughter looked at me wistfully and said, "It does not tell you what to do if it is quite impossible for you to ask your father." That is the sort of moment that tears at your heart.

But a few days later, something happened which showed that she had grasped something of deeper value—the meaning of communion, which is richer than communication can ever be.

We had returned from church one evening when she said that she had something to ask me. As she is completely unpredictable in her requests I said, "Well, what is it this time, Rosalind?" Then she said, with all the earnestness of a ten-year-old, "Last Sunday, and this Sunday again, in church I sat beside two old people. I do not think that they are very well, and I think that they might be lonely. If Daddy were here, and if he had been their minister, I expect we should have had them for tea. Can they come soon?"

I was rather taken aback as I did not really know these old folk, and I was not at all sure whether they would appreciate a visit to our home. But Rosalind was so insistent that I asked them, and joyfully they accepted.

After their visit Rosalind confided to me, "I expect you are thinking it was Jesus Who put the thought into my mind to ask these old folk to tea. I am sure He did. But I am sure also that Daddy had something to do with making me think about it."

I had never, to my knowledge, spoken to her about this communion, this fellowship of mind which she seemed to have grasped naturally and instinctively.

Just after Walter became convalescent in the days following his operation, he told me of some of his experiences during the dark, sorrowful days when his life was in grave danger. He said that he had an acute awareness in those days of the nearness of his own mother and my father, and he felt that they were both aware of his suffering, and by their sympathetic love for him were helping in Christ's ministry of succour and strength.

I was rather puzzled by this at the time because I was looking at it purely from the human point of view. I knew how Walter's sufferings tore at my own heart, and I liked to feel that those who had passed beyond this life would be free from such agonies. But then in pondering Walter's remarks I came to realise that those who are in Christ's presence see all our sorrow in the light of joy. They have a fuller knowledge than we have, and they know that pain will move on towards a higher purpose. If our loved ones know of our trials, then they also know of the triumph which will be ours in Christ, when the sorrow is past.

This, I think, is clarified for us in the Transfiguration, which I have already referred to. Moses and Elijah knew of Christ's approaching death, but they saw it in the light of His resurrection and ascension, and so their conversation with Him is of His coming "exodus", not of His coming sorrow.

Through Walter's experiences, when he himself was in the valley of the shadow, I came to be assured that if anything is able to withstand the shock of death, love is.

The writer to the Hebrews expresses something of what we mean by the Communion of Saints in his Epistle, chapter 12. Prior to this chapter, he has a splendid roll of honour full of the names of those who have served God faithfully, achieving great things and enduring terrible hardships; men and women who had won through to triumph.

There is a long list of people who are true exponents of faith in the Biblical sense. There are those who have won great victories through their faith, but there are also those mentioned who were "broken on the wheel"; some who were martyred; some who were compelled to suffer imprisonment and exile—a band of noble sufferers. To this impressive list we may add the names of our own contemporaries, for the roll of honour is not completed until it culminates in Christ, and includes all those who have followed, and those who do follow Him in faith. The full meaning of the names in the list can only be comprehended by reading the words at the end of it, in chapter 11: 40: "God . . . would not have them perfected, apart from us" (Moffatt).

Following this there is a challenge. "Wherefore, seeing we are encompassed by so great a cloud of witnesses . . ." The writer pictures us as running a race in an arena. On all sides around us as witnesses of our performance are those who themselves have been successful runners. They have joined the ranks of triumphant spectators.

It is salutary at this point to note that in the pursuit of our goal we are to have our eyes fixed—not on the witnesses, but on Christ Himself. Our ideal is to share in *His* triumph, and *His* glory, for the Christian life not only begins in Christ, but ends in Him. Still, the fact that we know and acknowledge the host of witnesses surrounding us is one of great comfort and strength.

The circle is immeasurably greater since the writer to the Hebrews envisaged it, and we can believe that in it are those known and loved by us. Fresh courage to endure comes to us when by faith we grasp this aspect of the great Communion of Saints.

What then is the Communion of Saints?

A saint is not just a person who has died, and gone to be with Christ. To Paul, every Christian, living or dead, was a saint. When he wrote to the Christians at Corinth he addressed them as saints even though many of them were blatantly and obviously far from perfect. As the New Testament understands it, everyone who lives for Christ, and in whom Christ lives, is a saint. There is a unity between those in whom the Spirit of Christ dwells, which is a unity for all time, not only in this life, but in the life beyond death.

Communion, as I have already indicated, is not communication. Even in this life a wordless communion between those who love each other is a much deeper and more precious thing than mere communication. The deepest fellowship, even on a human level, is a fellowship which involves the spirit—a mystic, sweet communion.

Many have found their trysting place with those whose rest is won at the Communion table. Here is the place which incorporates a memorial of the past with a fellowship in the present and a looking forward to the future. The Holy Communion, taken in its fulness, means a Holy Fellowship with Christ Himself, with our fellow-worshippers, with all the Church on earth, and with all the saints around the throne of God.

I have discussed this sense of nearness with many bereaved people, and to a great number it is a very real experience. But there are others who have written, or said to me, something like this: "If I could only experience the nearness of his presence, even in a dream, it would help. I have gone to sleep so often, hoping that in my dreams he would come to me, but he never has."

Others have said, "I have tried going to Communion, because you seem to indicate that there I should find a special awareness of a fellowship with those I have lost. But even there, I have felt no sense of nearness."

Without appearing to pass a harsh judgment, I think the first thing that needs to be emphasised once more is the importance of having our motives and our priorities right. Our primary motive in taking Communion should never be an attempt to create for ourselves an awareness of the presence of those who have died. Communion is a much greater Fellowship than that, and I think Christ's words would be to us, "Lovest thou Me more than these?" Christ must always be first in our thoughts, and in our prayers.

But, having said that, and knowing only too well the desires and cravings of the bereaved, I want to go on to say that we must not rely entirely on our *feelings* of nearness, or far-awayness. Some of us are, by nature and upbringing, far less perceptive than others where matters of the spirit are concerned. Because we do not *feel* a thing very deeply does not make that thing untrue. There are times when we are so crushed, so lonely, so depressed, so grief-stricken that it is difficult to believe anything very deeply.

When I have fleeting moments like that my mind invariably goes back to that scene in the garden after our Lord had risen. Mary was there, and she was weeping. The Lord, Who had been her companion, Who had given her strength for living, had died. She had come to the garden with spices, and had no doubt felt, in the way of bereaved people, that even to be near to the dead body of the One she had loved would bring solace and comfort. But now, she did not have even that meagre crumb. His body was gone. He seemed so very, very far away. Yet, in reality, He was never nearer to her than in that moment. He was right by her side, but, because of her grief and her tears, she did not realise or recognise His presence until He spoke to her by name.

Sometimes our loved ones seem so very far distant. But are they? If they are with Christ, and Christ is with us, then they cannot be very far away.

As I have been writing my children have had some friends in, and they have been trying out some new-found puzzles and tricks. One of these is deceptively simple. The children spread a flat piece of newspaper on the floor, and say to two of their friends, "We want you both to stand on this piece of paper in such a way that you cannot possibly touch each other." After numerous contortions and acrobatics and vehement assertions that the feat is not possible without tearing

97

the paper, my two girls give a sure demonstration that it can be done. They slide the piece of paper under the door, and shut the door over it. One of the girls remains on the outside, standing on her half of the paper, whilst the other remains inside the door on her half. They are resting on the one piece of paper, but the door between prevents tangible communication.

As I watched this game it seemed to me that a simple little parable had been enacted—a parable depicting the separation between ourselves, and those we love who have died. There is but a door between—the door that we call death. Though the door prevents tangible communication, yet our lives and theirs are not severed. There is a union and a fellowship still in Christ Jesus.

11

Resurrection of the Body

ONCE WE COME to the point of accepting that our dear departed are not in their final state, the question we all ask is, "What does the resurrection of the body really mean, and when will it take place?"

Sophisticated scorn has been poured upon this subject, not only in our own time, but in ages past, even in our Lord's day. The subject seems too vast for our human minds. Yet when we approach it with the humility of a little child, and look again at the world of Nature, we find that far from our observation hindering our faith, it enhances and develops it. We watch caterpillars spinning for themselves a sort of tomb, a chrysalis, a cocoon. If we were not knowledgeable or observant enough we should cast the rather ugly thing from us, thinking that that was in truth the end of the caterpillar. But in due course, from that rather unsightly and unattractive casing will emerge something exceedingly beautiful.

Or we see a shrivelled seed, nothing pretentious or imposing about it, so insignificant that in our ignorance we might toss it from us. Yet that same seed, embedded in the soil, will in due course produce a thing of colour and beauty, pulsating with life. The flower which emerges will bear small resemblance to the shrivelled seed which was its origin. God gives this merciful assistance to our faith.

Sometimes, in great sorrow, we have watched the slow failure of human capabilities in our loved ones. We have seen their vigorous energy replaced by feebleness. We have, with sorrow, seen a mind and memory, once alert and agile, become dim and wandering. We have seen eyes, which were once bright and perceptive, lose their lustre. In our folly, sometimes, because we equate these physical faculties with the whole person, we wonder how we could possibly believe in immortality, never mind the resurrection of the body.

But, though the outward man perish, yet is the inward man renewed. There is not one of us who has not had the privilege of knowing someone who, almost in inverse proportion to the decrease of physical powers, has increased in spiritual perception and growth.

The resurrection, or raising from the dead, is a fundamental doctrine of the Christian faith. It is a truth forcibly and clearly presented in Scripture, with its centre and ground in the Resurrection of Jesus Christ. Every New Testament book proclaims the Resurrection of Christ. It is the best attested fact in history, and on this fact is based the bodily resurrection of every Christian.

But, prior to Christ's Resurrection, the doctrine of bodily resurrection was taught. Indeed it was the chief article of controversy between the Pharisees and the Sadducees.

A company of Sadducees once approached Jesus trying to outpoint both Him and the Pharisees by showing, as they thought, the absurdity of a resurrection life. They thought it such a superficial doctrine that it would be easy to expose it. With some levity they posed a conundrum. If there were seven brothers, each having in succession the same woman as wife, she remaining childless in each marriage, whose wife would she be then in the resurrection?

Christ rebuked them in words which might also serve as a rebuke to us when we realise that so often our hesitant gropings are still hesitant gropings for precisely the same reason as the Sadducees. "Ye err, not knowing the Scriptures, or the power of God." We have not made it our business to become aware of what is Scripture's answer to our queries. And more, we have tried to reduce God to our own human level. We do not *know* the power of God. We limit the future, and all its possibilities, because we think of it only on the level of the life we know here and now.

Christ indicated quite clearly that questions based on earthly conditions are not really relevant to the resurrection life. If we are to approach Him sincerely with our enquiries, then we must be willing to reject all our materialistic conceptions of that life.

Christ's answer to the Sadducees was, "In the resurrection life, they neither marry, nor are given in marriage." On the face of it that seems but poor consolation to those of us who have been so happily married that we have thought of the marriage state as being the deepest and richest relationship we could possibly know. But life hereafter will not be any less rich or less full. It will just be different. All our relationships will be transfigured and transformed. Love, with its purest joys, will be restored to us, and some relationship nobler than marriage will be ours. "Eye hath not seen, nor ear heard, the things which God hath prepared for them that love Him" (1 Corinthians 2: 9).

Christ used words to the Sadducees which have proved words of comfort to those of us seeking truth about our departed friends. "I am the God of Abraham, and Isaac and Jacob—not a God of dead men but of living."

Martha was no Sadducee. When her brother Lazarus died, she made it quite clear, when talking to our Lord, that she believed in the resurrection of the dead. Admittedly, this was not of any immediate comfort to her in the rawness of her grief. Christ's consolation then to her, and to us now, are His words, "I am the Resurrection and the Life. He that believeth on Me, though he die, yet shall he live". The believer may experience physical death, but that does not mean that he has ceased to live.

Martha's belief about the final resurrection was based on Rabbinical teaching. Our belief is grounded on something incomparably stronger—the Resurrection of our Lord. Because this is of such vital importance to us all, in this life as well as in the life hereafter, I should like to deal with it at length in the next chapter.

Here I just want to assert that His Resurrection is the evidence and pledge of the resurrection of all His people. "Now is Christ risen from the dead, and become the first-fruits of them that slept" (1 Corinthians 15: 20). The "first-fruits" is a Jewish expression coming out of a Jewish custom which prevailed at the Feast of the Passover, or their Harvest Festival. Before the harvest was gathered an offering of the first fruits of grain was dedicated to God as the earnest, or pledge, of the full harvest to be reaped. The Resurrection of Christ is the pledge of the resurrection of all His followers.

Paul's teaching about the resurrection of the body is given in answer to people in Corinth who denied a bodily resurrection. Chapter 15 in 1 Corinthians, in which he expounds the doctrine, is one familiar to all who have attended a funeral service. But it is often only when the bereavement is personal, and the funeral service for a treasured companion that we come to study the argument and doctrine within the passage rather than merely allowing ourselves to be soothed and comforted by the words.

People ask today, as they did in Paul's day, sometimes in bewilderment, and out of deep anguish, "How are the dead raised, and with what body do they come?"

A great deal of the bewilderment arises because people try to imagine something like a gathering together of all the material particles which have constituted the human frame. It is still possible to encounter this confusion in people who, for instance, have an aversion to cremation.

During many of the early Christian persecutions the ashes of the bodies of the martyrs were cast into the nearest river, and the persecutors jeered, "Now see if they will rise again." This jeer was based on a false premise—certainly not one taught or held by the Christians themselves. It was based on the erroneous belief that the body would be preserved intact, and re-animated at the resurrection. But of course, the earthly body decays and turns to dust, and the constituents are resolved in the elements.

In the light of Scriptural teaching I can see no difficulty about cremation. When a body is laid in a grave the forces of Nature set to work to dissolve it. The worn-out fabric of the body slowly disintegrates. Cremation merely accelerates the process. If God can resurrect the martyrs who were burnt alive at the stake, He will be able to resurrect those whose remains have been cremated instead of buried. We must not be crudely materialistic in our vision of the resurrection life.

Erroneous thinking seeps in because it is so difficult for us to picture things except on the material level. Thus we equate the resurrection body with the human frame as we know it in this life. Paul distinctly says that the body we have here and now is *not* the one we shall have after the resurrection—though as the seed is linked with the new plant, so in some strange way will our earthly body be connected with our heavenly one. In spite of dissolution and difference, yet we shall be the same persons.

Here, in faith, we must fall back on the inexhaustible creative power of God. God fits His creatures for their own special environment. Fish are made so that they are at home in the water. Birds have bodies which enable them to fly in the air. Our earthly bodies are suitable for life on this planet, but clearly these bodies, with their carnal functions, are not suitable for life in the spiritual realm. God will give us resurrection bodies suitable for our life with Him in the higher world.

We shall, in some strange and subtle way, be connected with the self known upon earth, so that, in fact, we shall retain our own identity. Much is hidden from us here, but we do get a glimpse of the nature of our resurrection existence when we read of our Lord's appearances to His disciples after He rose again. Clearly He was recognisable to them, though not always at the beginning of their meetings. There seemed to be some kind of limitation put upon them. For instance, the eyes of the disciples on the Emmaus Road were "holden" so that He was not immediately recognisable. That limitation, whatever it is, will be removed when we no longer see through a glass darkly, as Paul describes it, but shall see face to face.

Christ's appearances would indicate that when we are resurrected, we shall be freed of the earthly bonds of time and space. Christ was able to appear in a room suddenly, without prior warning, even though the doors were locked.

From Paul's description of the resurrection body in 1 Corinthians 15, there are certain truths we can emphatically deduce. We shall be like Christ. This earthly body is subject to waste and decay. It wears out. The heavenly body will be imperishable—forever beyond the erosion of disease and death. This human frame is all too prone to dishonour and sin, but then we shall have a spiritual body which is pure and glorified. We know only too well the meaning of human frailty, but in the resurrection we shall have done with the weakness of the body. We shall be "raised in power". The animal body, as we know it, with its functions for maintaining and continuing human existence, will no longer be needed. We shall be clothed with a new spiritual body fitted for dwelling in a spiritual world.

Paul is reticent about how this change is effected. Just as the creation of the first man as an act of God the Creator is beyond human understanding, so this final act of the same God cannot be explained here and now.

We shall all be changed. We shall all be transformed. The change is not from life *within* a body to life *without* a body. It is from life *within* one type of body to life *within* a different and higher type of body.

There are some who feel it unnecessary to ponder the doctrine of the resurrection of the body. They say, "What does it really matter?" Obviously, if it was a belief incorporated in the Apostles' Creed, it must have been of vital importance to the early Church. I think probably the most important reason for the truth being incorporated in the Creed was the assertion of the complete redemptive work of Christ. We are saved both body and soul, to a full, rich and blessed life—what is often described in Scripture as Abundant Life.

For the bereaved the doctrine holds great comfort as it asserts the permanence of personality, and guarantees recognition.

I remember once asking Walter about this question of recognition. I said, "Are you really sure that we shall recognise one another when we are in Christ's presence?" With great assurance he quoted some words to me (the name of their author eludes me), "Do you think we shall be greater fools there than we are here?"

12

Endless is the Victory

IT IS FAIRLY OBVIOUS that most people do not find it easy either to think or talk about death. The majority of us are rather uncomfortable about it. And just because we are uncomfortable, we try to cover up with jokes about undertakers, and wreaths and corpses. We engage in this sort of joking about everything we fear—mental illness and death being perhaps the two most prominent topics. We seem to try to push the realities of these calamities from our minds by superficial humour.

But then the day comes when Death becomes a stark reality in our own homes, and the jokes turn sour on us. So we push the reality from us in another way, and instead of using the word "death" we cling to more sentimental phrases like "passing on", or "passing away".

In our more honest moments we are aware that if our Christian faith is as real as we claim it to be, then there should be no bogey or terror still to be passed; there should be no need to sentimentalise a situation which Christ has dealt with, and dealt with triumphantly. Paul, when writing to Timothy, uses strong words: "Jesus Christ hath abolished death" (2 Timothy 1 : 10). That for Paul was an inspired certainty. Can it be the same for us? Do we know anything of the exuberant, triumphant assurance which the apostles proclaimed? Have we accepted the words of Christ Himself: "If a man keep my saying, he shall never see death" (John 8: 51); "Whosoever liveth and believeth in Me, shall never die" (John 11: 26)?

What can we take from these words, words of our Lord Himself, except that the gloomy images with which we have surrounded death—the fears, the terrors, the "icy river", "the dark valley", are not the images He has sought to provide us with.

Christ teaches emphatically the indestructibility of life, if we are His. I find it difficult in the light of this to understand the attitude or beliefs of the people who will say they are convinced Christians, and yet who make a fetish of the grave where loved ones are buried. A memorial ought to be reverenced, a grave kept tidy and in order, but constant pilgrimages to the grave for what is within is not a Christian but a pagan practice. Only the mortal remains are within the earth, and the loved one, if he has trusted Christ, lives on. For the Christian, the grave must be nothing more than a memorial.

After the record giving the story of Christ's death we read some truly astonishing words. "Jesus was parted from them. . . . And they returned to Jerusalem with great joy, and were continually in the temple, praising and blessing God." This we can read at the end of Luke's Gospel.

Now compare the attitude and demeanour of these bereaved disciples with that of ourselves a few short weeks after our own bereavement. Should we not, judging them by our own feelings, have expected them to be utterly desolate, quite disconsolate, altogether woe-begone? Could we not imagine that they ought to be suffering, not only the pains of sorrow, but the bitterness of disillusion? Here they were with seemingly the wrecks and ruins of a great dream. The King whom they had expected to establish an earthly kingdom was parted from them. Yet their joy was great. Is it possible that we too can take things which, humanly speaking, have destroyed all our hopes and aspirations, and, by God's help, transform and transfigure them into situations which will cause us to praise and bless God.

The reason for the disciples' joy was, of course, the Resurrection. This is the fact which is the impregnable foundation of our own hope of life beyond the grave.

There can be no doubt at all about the authenticity of the resurrection. Some of the documents which provide the accumulation of evidence date back to within thirty years of the historical event. Paul tells us that when he wrote 1 Corinthians 15, there were many still alive who were witnesses of the event. Paul himself mentions five of the Lord's appearances, besides his own personal meeting with the Risen Lord on the road to Damascus. Altogether there are ten distinct appearances mentioned in the New Testament, not only to individuals, but to companies and crowds.

The appearances of Christ are first of all to the women, then to Peter; to the two men walking the Emmaus road; to the ten apostles, and then to the eleven; to seven men approaching the seashore; to all the apostles; to the five hundred brethren gathered together; then to James; and finally to the small group gathered round Him when He ascended.

Besides these definite records of Christ's appearances, every New Testament book declares or implies that Christ rose again. But the strongest and most convincing proof of all is the existence and growth of the Christian Church. The seeming catastrophe on Good Friday, and its immediate effects on disheartened disciples, must have been superseded by a great and mighty act. For instead of the weak and indecisive followers whom we see at the foot of the Cross, we meet men who could boldly and fearlessly, with an unembarrassed freedom of speech, face those who had condemned Christ, and could proclaim to them His Resurrection and His Lordship.

Belief in the resurrection is not just something we may add to our other Christian beliefs as a sort of appendage. It is the whole of the Christian faith. The very fact that we meet at all for worship every first day of the week is token of our belief that our Lord rose from the dead on the first day of the week, on that first Easter, nearly two thousand years ago. And by doing so defied and defeated death for us. We cannot present Christianity without presenting a Risen Christ.

Representatives of the great founders of religions have been, from time to time, depicted in characteristic poses. Some are pictured teaching, some reading, some meditating. Any one of these attitudes could portray Christ, but characteristically He is most often shown to us as a suffering Redeemer, nailed to a Cross. Yet the picture must not end there, for He was not only the sufferer. He was also the Victor—Victor over sin and suffering and death.

Here is our Christian hope—indeed the hope which is the exclusive claim of Christianity, for we can say without question that of all religions Christianity is the only one which has come to grips with death.

All through their lives the apostles declared, and declared confidently, that Christ had met them after His death, that He had conversed with them, that He had lived intermittently amongst them. It was the truth for which they were willing to accept banishment, exile, imprisonment and even violent death.

The evangelists in their records of the resurrection are very clear in pointing out that it was no ghostly apparition, no disembodied spirit that they had encountered. Christ Himself emphasised His own body, when He showed the apostles and His companions in Jerusalem the marks of His wounds. But it was a glorified body, wondrously transformed, and yet not altogether unrecognisable. Death and Resurrection had stripped Christ of the bonds of time and space which His earthly life had imposed upon Him. Within the space of a single evening the Lord had appeared to Peter at Jerusalem, and to Cleopas and his companion at Emmaus, and again to the disciples at Jerusalem in a room with locked doors. This is the Christ who can and does manifest Himself to us today.

It is comforting and interesting to note that each of those with whom He met was given a token by which they might recognise Him and receive assurance. Mary realised Who it was when He used her name. The two on the road to Emmaus recognised Him when He broke and blessed the bread. When He repeated a former miracle, filling the fishermen's net with fish, they joyously accorded Him recognition.

Sometimes people ask how we shall recognise our loved ones in their glorified state. Perhaps it is that those who have gone on ahead of us will recognise us first, and reveal themselves to us by some familiar token. Who knows? The real comfort for us lies in the words of Romans 6: 9: "Christ being raised from the dead dieth no more." Christ was raised with an immortal, incorruptible body, possessed of characteristics which will be forever exempt from death. And it is a similar body that we shall have at His return.

Our concern, like the disciples', should be to proclaim the resurrection of Christ, not to try to explain it. It is quite beyond our comprehension or knowledge. It is pure miracle, an act of God. It is the sign vouchsafed to us of God's ultimate victory over sin and death, and is in truth God's mightiest act.

The importance of the resurrection to the disciples can be judged by the place it had in their preaching. It was always in the forefront, even when they knew it would run counter to all the creeds and prejudices of the assembly they were addressing. The simple statement made by Paul, "If Christ hath not been raised, then is our preaching vain", reveals the importance—the all-importance—of the resurrection to him.

In the light of the resurrection, the Cross was more than just the tragic death of one who had lived a life of perfect example. The whole fabric of Christianity is woven round this central theme, "He is not here. He is risen."

I often wish we had the custom here which is observed in the Eastern Orthodox Churches where members greet each other with unashamed joy on Easter morning. "Christ is risen!" is the greeting. "He is risen indeed!" is the glad response. Here are the words which answer all the questions of seeking hearts, and provide the radiant glory of light which can flood into the bereaved soul, saying that sin, the grave and death have been vanquished. Here are the words which give glad, unutterable peace to the sorrowing. Life and immortality have been brought to light by the Risen Christ.

To any who have stood with those they love in the valley of the shadow of death, this is the great and glorious message of Easter. Christ is risen, and because He lives, we shall live also.

Once we are certain of the Risen Christ we change all our definitions of life and death. The disciples were absolutely certain their Lord was alive, and their vigour in proclaiming the Gospel after their meetings with Him enabled the stupendous news to spread throughout the known world. As someone has so aptly said, "Far from the Gospels explaining the Resurrection, it is the Resurrection which explains the Gospels." The disciples' knowledge of the Risen Christ changed the world.

So He can change us too, and all our approach to both life and death. When we really come to know Him we lose all our choking fear of the unknown. The values of eternity, as opposed to the values of earth, begin to be realised. To know Him is life eternal.

Access to Christ, since His resurrection, is universally complete. The poor can have Him always. The sick can enjoy the presence of the Divine Physician. The sorrowing can avail themselves of the Divine Comforter. Communion with Him is assured, both here and hereafter, for His parting promise was, "I will be with you alway, even unto the end of the world."

Our faith in the resurrection, however, to be a true faith, must be based not just on the evidences provided in the Scriptures, but on an individual experience of the power of the presence of the living Christ. No physical realisation of His presence is vouchsafed to us, but when we make the experiment of faith, when we "lay hold" of the living Christ for ourselves, then we know assuredly the confidence of victory, and the peace of soul which comes through knowledge of unity with Him and His purpose.

Sometimes, indeed very often, the experience of sorrow quickens our spiritual vision. Love for someone who is suffering, whom we feel powerless to help—such terrible stress of circumstances drives us to our knees. Even when a lifetime of hopes and plans is wrecked in one fell swoop, and our encounter with God is one of desperate questioning—even there can we meet the Living Christ. When we have shared a strange and secret sorrow with God in Christ, there is created a bond between us and Him which cannot be broken. And when we let Him share in our sufferings to the extent that we allow Him to offer us triumph and hope through His resurrection, there is a unity and fellowship with Him which is forged for all eternity.

13

Punishment . . .

I CAN REMEMBER that when I used to talk to Walter about the life hereafter, and about those who will inherit the rewards of heaven, there were several things about which he was very definite and very forceful.

The first point that he would emphasise was this. It is not for us to judge who is outside the pale of salvation. He felt that too often human beings set limits on the power of God's love to enter a man's life. He maintained (and the longer I live, the more I believe this) that no human being can possibly know fully what transactions have gone on between another human being and his Maker. Walter used to say to me, "We shall have many surprises when we are in the company of the redeemed. Not all who have said 'Lord, Lord' will be there. But many we have never recognised as His will be rejoicing in His presence." I am sure it is true that many of the verdicts made, many of the judgments passed by men, will be reversed.

It is of course right that we should be concerned, not only about our own salvation, but very deeply about that of other people. Yet many of our doubts about those we love are not so much doubts of them, but doubts about Christ Himself.

> *Trust Him though thy sight be dim.*
> *Doubt for them is doubt of Him.*

The second thing about which Walter used to express concern was the obvious enjoyment with which some preachers he knew proclaimed the doctrine of eternal punishment. He believed without a doubt in this eternal separation from God, but he often said to me, "We should never preach about it unless we can do so with a breaking heart." He believed there should be no jubilation over the fate of the wicked.

He was concerned, not only for a man's congregation, but for the man himself when he heard denunciatory and threatening sermons; strident harangues where the preacher, with some sadistic relish, pictured his rebellious hearers in the torments of hell. He said to me, "How can any Christian paint such gruesome and hideous terrors, and then come away from the service, casual and uncaring, able to eat a hearty supper, thinking little of the tortured hearers left behind?" His own aim was, believing in the judgments of God, not to terrify men into acceptance of Christ, but by love to persuade them.

But he was a realist. He had just as little patience with those who sluggishly rejected the idea of eternal punishment just because it offended their easy-going, lazy, good-natured approach to wrong-doing.

He proclaimed that the realism of Christ and Christianity is just this—the ugly facts of life both here and hereafter must be faced for what they are. There are sharp edges to truth which we should not seek to blunt: bitter pills which we should not seek to sugarcoat.

We cannot soften Christ's warnings, or the severity of His language, when He spoke about unrepented sin. It is sheer sentimentalism to seek to do so, and it distorts all His teaching, and that of His apostles.

It is not very fashionable these days to talk about retribution. We realise, perhaps more than ever, the fallibility of human judgment. We realise that often to know all is to for-give all. Of course, it is perfectly right and proper that human judgment should be regarded as fallible. But when we think of judgment in the Biblical sense, we are not thinking in terms of human judgment. God, the Divine Judge, can be trusted to administer perfect justice.

We are responsible people, and as such are answerable to God for our thoughts and actions which we (most of us) would readily admit are within our human powers to control.

The many questions we would like to ask about eternal punishment are not all answered for us in the New Testament. But there is sufficient knowledge given to us to act as a warn-ing, and to enable us to approach the subject with a proper sense of awe and responsibility. The entire question of eternal life, or eternal punishment, must be viewed in the light of the total revelation of God and His love.

One thing is explicit from Scriptural teaching. Just as eternal life in the presence of Christ is the full realization of what men have begun for themselves on earth, so eternal separation from God is the full realization of what men have chosen for themselves in this life. What the material con-ditions of a type of existence hereafter, separate from God, could mean are comparatively unimportant. What is im-portant is that Christ and His apostles viewed eternal separa-tion from God as a reality. Men choose Heaven or Hell before they ever reach there. As Godet, the great Biblical commentator, has said, "It is not so much that in Heaven we are to find God, but in God we are to find Heaven."

The fact, once realised, that we must all appear one day before God our Judge should create within each one of us a sense of awed responsibility. We need to regain that sense of awe, and that sense of responsibility, in these modern times when we have ceased largely to include that word "sin" in our vocabularies. And when, in fact, we have ceased largely to fear and reverence God as He ought to be feared and reverenced.

Today delinquent behaviour is wrapped up in a more attractive package than when the plain word "sin" was written on the label. "Sin" is sugarcoated, treated as a "complex", "a disease", "psychopathic behaviour". We must, of course, thank God for the more sympathetic approach to the sinner which is to be found in so many quarters today. And we must remember unceasingly that God must often see sin where we see no sin; and very often, with His infinitely greater wisdom and knowledge, He must see no sin, or completely forgiven sin, where we are hasty to condemn.

Acknowledging all that, it is still very possible to remain indifferent through a too-sentimental, goodwill, easy-going approach to the problems of sin. Our consciences can become sluggish and indolent. It is all too easy to reach the stage—a dangerous stage—where we cease to condemn anything in thought or behaviour in either ourselves or others. To exonerate everyone is in the end to exonerate no-one. Whilst stating emphatically that God is the final judge, yet He has set us explicit moral standards which we transgress at our peril. Christ's compassion for the sinner did not mean any compromise with sin itself.

Sin has its inevitable sequel in pain and suffering and punishment. Conduct has its consequences. God is King and Judge now—not just King and Judge at the Last Day. He has been King and Judge from the beginning. He is eternally reigning and eternally judging. In every human crisis, and in every crisis in history, His judgment has been evident. Indeed the word "crisis" is the Greek word for "judgment". The consummation of all these crises will come at the end of history when Christ will come again, with glory. Then, according to Scripture, we may expect a visible manifestation of Christ on earth, with a triumphant demonstration of the salvation of all who have faith in Him, and the destruction of those who have persisted in rebellion. This dramatic finale is spoken of repeatedly in Scripture.

The truth which is eminently clear from Scriptural teaching is that when men wilfully disregard what knowledge of God they possess, there is inevitable punishment. It is not lack of knowledge which condemns men. It is obduracy of heart.

Real life consists of a living relationship with Christ. Real death means an absence of relationship with Him. Penalty for unforgiven sin means separation from Christ. Those who have loved darkness rather than light have in fact chosen an existence separate from the life in Christ which God offers to us all.

We must somehow reconcile what the Bible teaches about God as Judge, and what it teaches about God as Love. The reconciliation does not come about by ignoring the dreadful question of eternal punishment. It comes in looking again at the Cross of Christ. Here it is that God shows, with unutterable pain and love, His concern for erring mankind, and His hatred of sin. Here also we see His longing to reconcile the sinner to Himself. So it is at the Cross that we can see God as Love, and also God as Judge.

When this knowledge of God has been vouchsafed to us, we should live in untiring preparedness for the moment of crisis, of judgment. This does not imply a perpetual state of stress, but rather a complete and wholehearted committal to the Lordship of Christ so that there will be a continual choosing of God before self, of good before evil.

In the light of this the really critical moment for any human being is not the moment of bodily death. It is the moment when we die to self and live unto God; the moment when we become unashamedly and wholeheartedly His. The life after death will then become for us but a joyous continuation of the life in Christ which we know here and now.

14

And Reward

THERE ARE those who say that to live here and now in such a way as to have the hope of immortality hereafter is a selfish hope. It need not be. The craving of the soul for all that is noble and pure and good is not so much a craving for unceasing happiness and reward for oneself, but a deep longing to see all that is incomplete made complete, all that is imperfect perfect, and to know Love in all its fulness.

C. S. Lewis once preached a sermon in St. Mary's University Church, Oxford, which was afterwards published by S.P.C.K. under the title *The Weight of Glory*. In this sermon he said that the Lord seemed to find our desires for reward not too strong, but too weak.

Certainly Christ was not shy of the word REWARD.

Great is your reward in heaven (Matthew 5: 12).

He shall in no wise lose his reward (Matthew 10: 42).

Do good ... and your reward will be great (Luke 6: 35).

Nevertheless, our love for God demands a radical obedience to Him, irrespective of reward. Those who have entered into true fellowship with God know that any rewards hereafter are no mere bribes to encourage them to acknowledge His Lordship. They are rather a challenge. Life with Christ in Heaven will be the consummation of all our earthly discipleship, and we have a great reward here, as well as hereafter, in just knowing Him. For to know Him is, in truth, Life Eternal.

Life in Heaven is quite beyond our imagination or comprehension. All that we can really grasp is that then all imperfection will have passed. Our imaginations are necessarily limited by our present thoughts of time and space. But we believe that God's plan for the individual, and for the world as a whole, is the perfection of all creation. All the imperfections of the present order will have passed, and Light, Love, Joy and Righteousness will be the basic constituents of the new life with Christ.

Having said that, however, it seems quite clear that conduct has its consequences, even for the Christian who has entered into a right relationship with God through faith in Jesus Christ. There is seemingly in God's new order a place for reward for works. Before our entrance to that new, that perfect Life, we must each pass before the Judgment Seat of Christ. Our faith in Christ does not mean that we are exempt from that.

When I used to talk to Walter about the Judgment of Christ, he told me he tended to believe—though no one can be emphatic—that we meet Christ as Judge when we leave this world at death. He said that he believed that every wrong not righted in this life we would be required to make right in the life to come. Though we cannot be emphatic about when our judgment will be, on one point we can be dogmatic—we shall all be judged.

It seems that the more sensitive we become to the claims of God, so the more aware we are of our imperfections. We are so very conscious that our life here is but a probationary prelude to our life hereafter. Then we know that we shall see ourselves in our true worth, and our deepest motives will be laid bare. But we need not be weighed down entirely by a negative sense of failure and folly, for one of the great and comforting paradoxes of the Christian religion is that if Christ is our Judge, He is also our Advocate.

It is often asserted that Paul and James are at variance on the question of faith and works. I think William Barclay, in his studies on James,[1] hits the nail on the head when he says that it is not so much that they are at variance as that they use different starting points. Paul begins at the very beginning, asserting that no man can earn the forgiveness of God. A man can only accept forgiveness as a free gift, offered in Christ. James, on the other hand, begins later with the professing Christian. No man can be saved by works. But once he professes salvation, once he claims to be in a right relationship with God, then his Christianity must be shown by his works.

Paul, I think, is often misrepresented on this question of faith and works, and his doctrine is often misunderstood. On a great many occasions he laid stress on the ethical effect of Christianity. He speaks in Romans 2: 6 of God rendering to every man according to his deeds. Again in Romans 14: 12 he emphasises that every one of us shall give account of himself to God. In 2 Corinthians 5: 10, Paul warns that we must all appear before the Judgment Seat, each to be requited for what he has done on earth, be it well or ill.

The truth that seems prominent throughout is that, though we are saved by faith, we are rewarded according to our works. Our lives will be tested in the Day of the Lord. Then the rewards will be made known.

What these rewards will be is not clear, but we are given some indication even here and now of the joy to be reached through a life of service. Perhaps the greatest is just in knowing Christ, and experiencing something of the Life Eternal in communion with Him. To have Christ is in truth to have

[1] Published by the Church of Scotland.

everything. We can at the moment only picture our relationship with Him in human terms. And surely all that we know here and now is puny indeed when compared to the bliss which will be vouchsafed to us hereafter.

There will be the reward of approval when we hear the words, "Well done, thou good and faithful servant." What great pleasure will be experienced as the creature becomes aware of the approval of His Creator. This is where I believe humility will be perfected.

There will be the reward of knowledge. Then we shall know, even as we are known. We shall no longer see as through a glass darkly. We shall see face to face.

There will be the reward of glory. In the Old Testament, glory generally refers to a revelation of God, as in Isaiah's vision. Always when glory is spoken of there is implied a realisation of all the radiance and power of God. When we come to the New Testament, this revelation includes that of God in Christ, as when Paul met Christ on the Damascus Road. Surely in the life hereafter, one of the rewards will be a sharing in this glory and radiance.

We can find numerous references to this glory in Scripture. In Daniel 12: 3 we read, "They that be wise shall shine as the brightness of the firmament." Matthew 13: 43 says, "The righteous shall shine forth as the sun." In Colossians 3: 4 the words are, "When Christ, Who is our life, shall be manifested, then shall we also be manifested in glory" (R.V.).

In the sermon of C. S. Lewis, to which I have already referred, he warned that in the end the Face, which is the delight or terror of the universe, must be turned on each one of us, either conferring glory inexpressible or inflicting shame that can never be disguised.

Nowadays we tend to turn away from pomp and circumstance. The idea of splendour and glory and pageant is abhorrent to many a modern mind. Certainly not many of us now regard as our idea of bliss a city paved with gold, and a company with white robes and harps and crowns. Those of us who live in a prosaic age must not allow ourselves to be deterred by the poetry of Biblical language. There is a wealth of imagery here, indicating that somehow we shall be united with all that is beauty, grace, and power.

Further, there is the reward of further service to Christ, as illustrated in Christ's parable of the stewards. When I returned to teaching I was immensely struck on lifting a small arithmetic book to see each page divided into two sections. At the bottom half of each page were little problems labelled, "For the quicker pupils."

The reward for completing the first half of the page was not to be allowed to sit back with folded arms, doing nothing. It was to be set further, more interesting problems to work out. And indeed, those of us who teach know that there is nothing so intolerable to industrious and conscientious children as to be left in idleness. They abhor it. To keep them happy means to keep them busy.

So, though we often use words like "rest from our labours" about the life hereafter, we do not mean enforced idleness. We mean rather a removal of the stresses and tensions which rob us of real joy in our labours and tasks. To have proved ourselves in God's sight, as able stewards, is to be given further, more exacting work to complete for Him. We are not exactly sure what this may mean, but it seems that we shall have some part to play in His Universe. We shall be sharers in God's own glory and kingdom.

The Holy City is the place where despair is unknown; pain is abolished; all the consequences of sin are removed. Grief and pain and death are absent. But more than this absence, this negative bliss, there is the glorious presence of

Christ Himself, and all that His glory will bring to us in the ecstasy of union with Him. This is the greatest joy of Heaven. The clear vision and true knowledge of God is reward enough.

C. S. Lewis ended his famous sermon by saying that though we might get to the place of thinking too much of our own potential glory hereafter, we cannot think too often or too deeply about that of our neighbour. Every relationship becomes more valuable in the light of what each person may one day be in Christ's presence.

In our human weakness we must admit that the thing we most often long for in heaven is the joy and reward of meeting those who have gone on before us. Our love for God is scarcely pure enough, or holy enough, to desire Him above those we have loved here on earth. But as we come to know Him better and worship Him more fully, we know that to dwell in the love and the presence of God is to have everything else besides.

We are impatient for the day when our joy will be complete. When our griefs tend to overwhelm us, we are conscious of a burning wistfulness for that time when our tears will be wiped away, and sorrow will be forgotten.

> *My God, I can wait*   *If Thou uphold me:*
> *I can endure*   *If Thou sustain me:*
> *I can give up*   *If Thou reward me:*
> *I gladly will do all*   *If Thou command me:*
> *O righteous Judge, Thou art both strong and patient,*
> *I will be patient if Thou make me strong.* (6) [1]

[1] Copies of this prayer are obtainable from St. Mary's Press, Wantage, Berks.

15

Can We Take It?

LATE ONE AFTERNOON I was travelling homewards in a hospital
bus after visiting one of my children who was ill. I sat
beside a young woman who had been visiting her very sick
husband in hospital. She told me that her mother was also
lying gravely ill at home. She said they had a fine minister
whose reputation was high in his care for the sick and the
dying. "But," she remarked, "I have written to him and
asked him not to come to visit Mother, because if she saw
him she would realise that she was dying. I don't want her
to know. She just couldn't take it."

The woman was a complete stranger to me, and the bus
journey far too short to enter into any deep discussion. But
afterwards I was much perturbed at my failure to come to
grips with the matter in the available few minutes. It was
so apparent that here was another instance of someone who
was quite unwilling to face the reality of death for herself,
or for those she loved.

Round about the same time I was engaged with some other
folk in our church in a house-to-house visitation of people
whose children came to Sunday school, but who themselves
took no interest in the church. I knocked at one door, and
the father of the family answered. I asked if I might talk to
him and his wife together. I was told that she was very ill,

so I suggested that we might ask the minister to call. I shall never forget the look of consternation on the father's face. "Oh, whatever you do, don't do that!" he exclaimed. "She's not as ill as all that, and I wouldn't like her to get the impression she was dying."

Here again was this strange, and all too prevalent, notion that religion is only for the dying—the tacit admission that when life is nearly over we may have some need for the succour and strength which Christ offers. But this job of everyday life—that is a different matter. We do not need Him *now*—or so many of us like to think. Death and bereavement does not yet fit into our scheme of things, or our way of thinking.

Few of us take the trouble to train ourselves to cope with sorrow and suffering and loss. We become complacent and uncaring when things go too well with us for too long, and—God forgive us—we so often become blind to the sufferings and needs of others.

When severe illness, sorrow and bereavement come, do we really know how to handle it? The Christian faith is realistic, and faces the reality of death. We are taught through this faith that *now* is the time to think about death. For once we die to self and live unto God then physical death has lost a great deal of its terror.

I do not want to give the impression that those who trust God do not have any moments of fear or apprehension. This would be to blind oneself to the facts. There are dark days. We are all subject to human frailty. We have our moments of sure and certain hope, and then our times of weakness and uncertainty when we go stumbling blindly about to find the truth again.

Christ had His own spiritual struggles, especially in the Garden of Gethsemane. It is helpful for us to remember that even the Christ of God asked that His cup of suffering should be removed from Him. He has passed the same troubled road as ourselves, and He fully understands our struggles and our weaknesses. He was the Son of God. Because of this, He had an infinitely deeper experience of grief than we can ever know. But His path of sorrow led to glory and triumph. With Him as our companion our path of sorrow can lead to glory and triumph too.

Even sorrow can be found to be a disguised gift, and bereavement not all loss. So often through these griefs we find that God has helped us to develop spiritual maturity. What at first seems to be the darkest moment of our lives can be found later to be suffused with Divine radiance and glory.

No one can understand how it is that God communicates to us the Christ-life which transforms every situation—even those which seem to have made wreck and ruin of all our human hopes and aspirations. But it is true that directly we submit to Him as Lord, then, by some inexplicable process, He comes into our lives to live and reign. This is something we cannot imitate, or create for ourselves. But it is essential to remember that, "Unless we crown Him Lord of all we do not crown Him Lord at all."

There are some things we learn, through Christ, which help us not only to live, but to face the prospect of dying. Two of these things we have only begun to understand here and now. One is the power of Love, and the other is the power of Prayer.

Without question Love is the most important force in the life of any human being. Deprive a child of it, and he is starved in a far more terrible and emaciating way than if he were deprived of material food. His mind will become warped; his personality stunted. To open our hearts to love, both human and divine, and to offer love in return, is to open our lives to fulness and growth.

Love helps us to live. Love also gives us the courage to die—in the sure knowledge that such love as we have experienced, even on the human level, can never die.

"I go to My Father." This was how Christ spoke of His death to His disciples. This was the thought He used to steady them when the time of His departure was approaching. For those who have loved God this is what death should mean—a going out to a loving Father; not departure, but arrival; not a sleep, but a true awakening.

The power of prayer is another mystifying influence in our lives. When we link our lives with the power of the Divine through prayer, we cannot tell what immense achievements are ahead of us in His strength. We have all within us, I believe, far more patience and courage than we are generally called upon to use. When we allow these human resources to be linked to His eternal resources then there is power untold.

These truths about love and prayer are not new truths. Christ, in His Sermon on the Mount, and indeed throughout His earthly ministry, showed what inestimable value He placed on both love and prayer. To-day it seems that some of these old truths are being rediscovered. At least the truth about Love is being rediscovered scientifically through psychiatry and psychology. We are being taught that it is impossible to love without life being greatly enriched, and that to withhold love is to impoverish life.

Just as love and prayer can enrich life, so they can take away much of the terror of death. Love and prayer can give a human being the unshakeable strength to face grave illness and suffering. God's power is inexhaustible, and it is available to us in our hour of deepest need. Our lives remain miserably undeveloped when our hearts and minds are not attuned to the Infinite.

If we allow love and prayer to be the energising influences in our lives, then we are going along the right road towards finding true joy and peace which are not to be found in circumstances, but inwardly in the heart.

Peace and joy can come to us, even in sorrow, as an inward serenity—but only when we are in a right relationship with God. This is not an experience which ignores the disquiet of the world; the hunger of the souls around us; the sorrows of mankind. In fact, it is only when we are in a right relationship with God in Christ that we see these things aright. The blindfolds are taken off.

Peace and joy do not mean merely freedom from anxiety and stress and strain. They mean something positive in a negative situation, and they can come only through communion and union with Christ. Even in the midst of conflict and sorrow we can be aware that our lives are linked with Christ, and a victorious Christ at that. This means more than just an acceptance of Christ's teaching; more than just a belief that His claims are just. It is a whole-hearted committal of self-will, intellect and emotions—so that an indestructible relationship with Him is built for eternity.

Joy is one of the great legacies which Christ has bequeathed to us. "That my joy might be in you, and that your joy might be complete." We do not know fully that completeness of joy as yet. There is a sense of imperfection in our experience of it. But there is the sure knowledge that when Christ shall come our joy will be complete, indestructible, perfect. Joy is a by-product of our relationship with God, and it is something which is assuredly not at the mercy of circumstances. Even when a lifetime of hopes and plans is wrecked in one fell swoop, we can still know that our treasure is in the Saviour's keeping, and that we can find it again in His arms.

Christ has revealed Himself to us as an abiding spiritual presence, available to each one of us—if we really desire Him enough. Sometimes bereaved people have said to me that in the bitterness of their grief God seemed to have turned a deaf ear to their pleas for His presence. Yet when we have sat down to analyse the situation, we have found that it was not that God had not revealed Himself. It was rather that they had been unable to realise or recognise His voice or His presence. Sometimes He tries to speak to us through a wise and loving counsellor or friend. We are not always willing or ready to recognise His voice when He speaks through other people. We are not always willing to grasp His hand when others offer, in His name, their friendship and help. We are not always willing to acknowledge His love when it is showered upon us by other warm, human hearts.

In Christ's hour of greatest loneliness and suffering He was careful to remember His own sorrowing mother. No doubt she had already suffered bereavement as it would seem that Joseph had predeceased Christ. Jesus thought of her as she stood broken-hearted at the foot of the Cross. He commended her to the care of John. "Son, behold thy Mother. Mother, behold thy son." In His mercy He makes provision for each one of us too.

When Christ comes to us in our happiness, He is greater than the greatest happiness we can possibly experience. And when He comes to us in sorrow, His coming is the compensation for all our grief. I know.

16

God Holds the Key

IT IS now over four years since my little private world collapsed around me; since I realised with devastating awareness that one chapter of my life had been completed, and that nothing could be quite the same again. One never completely overcomes that sense of "aloneness" when one is very conscious of the incompleteness of a home in which a loved partner is not to hand to share in all that home-making involves.

Yet despite the awareness of being alone there is, paradoxically, the mysterious absence of the feeling of loneliness in the usual way that we think of loneliness. I have been so conscious, as I think my children have too, of the continuing abiding presence of Christ. He was the One Who came to meet us in the dark valley, and Who led us through triumphantly to the light again. He is the One Who has helped us to readjust to a new way of life, for readjustments there must be. The widowed and fatherless must accept that all life after their bereavement is a daily problem of making adjustments.

It has not been easy these past four years. There have been times when the turbulence of passion and the waywardness of the human will have made me aware that as human beings we are never entirely fortified against the injury of the soul and the corrosion of the heart which the storms of calamity and disappointment often bring. Just as perishable materials need to have their protective coverings constantly renewed, so we need to submit ourselves continually to the shielding, fortifying love of God.

I can remember one week of terrible bewilderment and mental turmoil. It was just a few weeks after Walter's death. Every plan I seemed to have made collapsed around me, and chaos seemed to reign.

The first chink in my armour appeared one morning when the post arrived, bringing a card for Michael from the Chest Clinic. He had attended for his regular check-up and X-ray just a few days previously, and he had seemed very fit and well. I had assumed that the X-ray would be clear, but now there was a card recalling him for further examination. I trembled at the prospect of more pain and distress and illness, for I immediately assumed that the emotional disturbance of his father's death had caused a relapse.

Michael, at 14, was calmer than I was. He went off to school, saying that he would call in at the Clinic at break time. "I expect that something has gone wrong with the machine or the film," he said philosophically. Whether he really felt as calm as he sounded, I never really got round to asking him.

After he had gone I decided to 'phone the clinic to enquire about the recall. There I received the reassuring news that it was simply due to a technical hitch. I was too relieved to berate the people concerned for not making this clear on the card. It would have been so easy to do so, and I know now that I was not the first—or the last—to be caused unnecessary panic through a similar detached notice of recall from a clinic or hospital.

The occasion was, however, of some value. It taught me

that my equilibrium and resilience were not quite what I imagined them to be. I had, I discovered, very little within myself upon which I could rely. I was only strong when every moment I was leaning upon Christ. The experience revealed some points of weakness still—a revelation which drove me even closer to Christ. I remembered Walter's words to me the night he knew that nothing more could be done for him. He had said, "You are strong, darling. God keep you so, always."

Later that week I was to become even more conscious of my complete and utter need of Christ. We were all quite confident that we ought to remain in Scotland after Walter died—the country which had been home to the family for a number of years. We were happy among the Scots, and the children were benefiting under the Scottish system of education. Everything pointed to our remaining if only we could find a suitable house to rent. Indeed we had high hopes of being able to do so—until one morning when the 'phone rang and I heard, to my dismay, that every possibility in this direction had fled. All our hopes and plans for re-housing were smashed without warning in what seemed a cruel and callous manner. That was a painful moment of despondency and dejection. I was so emotionally fatigued after Walter's illness and death that I was quite unable to think clearly for a few days.

Then there came a dawning awareness that I had never really consulted God about where we should live. I had just assumed that since all circumstances pointed to Scotland that must be His plan for us. Now I began to question, and to ask if perhaps we had to learn the hard way that we were meant to return to my native Ireland.

Educationally there would be many difficulties in moving. Only those who have been obliged to change localities in these small islands of ours can realise just how frustrating the problems can be. The differences can be quite fantastic. Even the age limits for such things as what is erroneously called "the eleven plus" vary from one part of the country to another. Quite real and definite hardships are created for both the parents and children involved. Indeed, for the first months after I returned to Ireland, I wondered many times if I had interpreted God's will aright. Obstacle after obstacle seemed to present itself.

Many times during the first eighteen months or so the future seemed very obscure as the children and I battled with the many problems of readjustment. Often I would have to repeat to myself the words,

> *God holds the key of **all unknown**,*
> *And I am glad.*
> *If other hands should hold the key,*
> *Or if He trusted it to me,*
> *I might be sad.*

The *one thing* a widow must seek to prevent herself doing is falling in love with her troubles so that she becomes aware only of the hardships in her life. Her very position can give her a feeling of self-importance so that she feels others should be rushing constantly to her aid. She needs to beware of using her sorrows as a sort of emotional blackmail to make others feel under an obligation to give constantly of their time and thought to her particular problem. We can become too conscious of ourselves and our trials. Life is far too short to spend it licking our wounds. There is a battle still to be fought.

After a time things began to take shape. I had been appointed to a permanent teaching post. I was grateful for this, but I became increasingly aware that teaching for a young, widowed mother can produce an unnatural existence where there is very little time for adult companionship. All the working day is spent among children. In the evening we return home to a houseful of children needing double the attention because father is not present to share the parental responsibilities. It is very necessary to ensure that somehow there is time left for fellowship of a spiritual and intellectual kind with adult contemporaries. However charming children are, the mother's life and mental development could become stunted unless adult friendships are nurtured and encouraged.

On the credit side, of course, teaching is a most suitable occupation for a widowed mother. She finishes each day at the same time as her own children who need her at home. She has virtually the same holidays as they have. And the job is a reasonably secure one.

Our association with children too can often enable us to feel the nearness and beauty of heavenly things. I can remember the first Christmas after I had commenced teaching. (It is always the first time of doing anything after a bereavement which is so difficult—the first family holiday, the first birthday, the first anniversary, the first Christmas.) I was longing for the first Christmas season to be over, for I guessed there would be many wistful longings and many heartaches as we looked at the vacant chair.

As the day drew near I gathered my class round me and told these eight-year-olds the story of the shepherds on the hills around Bethlehem. I had reached the part where the angel of the Lord appeared to them, and I had just said the words, "And then the angel said . . .", when quite spontaneously the class recited in unison the words, "Fear not, for behold I bring you good tidings of great joy, which shall be to all people. For unto you is born this day, in the city of David, a Saviour which is Christ the Lord." It could not have been more effectively rendered if it had been rehearsed.

It is difficult to put into words what that small incident meant to me. I seemed somehow aware, as never before, of the heavenly radiance of that first Christmas out in the fields beyond Bethlehem. Facing the joyous season without Walter seemed to be not quite so difficult afterwards.

In time many of the educational difficulties regarding my own children were ironed out. Indeed, some of these were solved, where Michael was concerned, in ways which were beyond my wildest dreams. After about a year and a half in Ireland he was accepted into a school, some distance from home, which had great traditions and a very fine reputation. Not only that, but during term time he was invited to live in a home where the influence was wholly beneficial; where in his formative years he had access to the wisdom and guidance of a fine father and mother of a family of four. We were beginning to see in truth that if God takes away, then, from His fulness and His goodness, He will surely repay.

As I write this Michael is completing a year in Africa, where he is working voluntarily amongst African, Asian and European youth, pending his entry into university. It would seem as if he is fulfilling what his father's ambitions and hopes and ideals for him would be. The patterns of readjustment are beginning to fit into a picture which is not yet fully revealed, but which will, in time, I am sure, show an integrated plan.

The obstacles in our lives are not all overcome, but we are learning, with God's help, how to live with our grief. To have, to love, to lose, and then again to find. That is the sequence we believe. When circumstances are hard and adverse, yet God is greater still. We know assuredly that nothing can separate us from the love of God which is in Christ Jesus—neither death nor life, nor angels, nor principalities, nor powers, nor things present, nor things to come, nor height, nor depth, nor any other creature.

When sorrow and loss do tend to overwhelm there is a prayer written by Bishop Brent for the bereaved which never fails to bring healing and solace:

We give them back to Thee, dear Lord, Who gavest them to us. Yet as Thou dost not lose them in giving, so we have not lost them by their return.

Not as the world giveth, givest Thou, O Lover of souls. What Thou gavest, Thou takest not away; for what is Thine, is ours always, if we are Thine.

And Life is eternal, and Love is immortal, and death is only a horizon, and a horizon is nothing, save the limit of our sight.

Lift us up, strong Son of God, that we may see farther. Cleanse our eyes that we may see more clearly. Draw us closer to Thyself, that we may know ourselves nearer to our beloved, who are with Thee. And while Thou dost prepare a place for us, prepare us for that happy place, that where they are, and Thou art, we too may be.

Through Jesus Christ our Lord, Amen. (7)

Acknowledgments

I am most grateful to those publishers and authors who have given me permission to quote from copyright material. In one or two instances I have been unable to trace the source or owner of copyright, but should either my publisher or myself learn of these, then due acknowledgment will be given in the next edition.

1. Chapter 1, page 19.
   I am indebted to Hodder and Stoughton, London, for permission to use *Into The Woods* by Sidney Lanier. This poem is included in Arthur Mee's anthology *One Thousand Beautiful Things*.

2. Chapter 2, page 24.
   I wish to thank Sir Robert Platt, Professor of Medicine at the University of Manchester, and also the Editor of *The Lancet* for allowing me to use this excerpt from an article "Ageing and Death" written by Sir Robert and published in *The Lancet* on Jan. 5th, 1963.

3. Chapter 3, page 30.
   This short excerpt from Robert Frost's poem *Stopping by Woods on a Snowy Evening* is used by permission of Laurence Pollinger Ltd., London.

4. Chapter 5, page 52.
   My grateful thanks to William Collins Sons and Co., Ltd., and to Sydney Walton, Esq., C.B.E., M.A., B.Litt., St. James's Court, Buckingham Gate, the author's Executor, for permission to quote from Alexander Irvine's *My Lady of the Chimney Corner*.

5. Chapter 8, page 79.
   Mrs. Ann Armstrong and the Editor of *The Guardian* have kindly given permission for me to use this part of Mrs. Armstrong's article, published in *The Guardian*, Dec. 30th, 1963.

6. Chapter 15, page 125.
   This prayer was written by Bishop Frere of The Community of the Resurrection at Mirfield. It is printed on his prayer leaflet *Suspiria Animae Vix Amantis Deum*, and published by St. Mary's Press, Wantage, Berkshire, from whom copies can be obtained.

My thanks are due to both the Fathers of the Community and to the Sisters of St. Mary's Press for permission to reprint.

7. Chapter 16, page 138.
Bishop Brent, who wrote this prayer, was a United States Army Chaplain during the First World War. He is now deceased and I am grateful to his sisters in the U.S.A. who have given me permission to quote. The prayer is obtainable on prayer cards from St. Michael's House, Wantage, Berks.

E. U.